Championship Carving

by Tricia Veasey and Tom Johnson

Schiffer Publishing Ltd

Lem Ward Decorative *(From the collection of Dr. Kramer)*

Other books from the Veasey family.

Waterfowl Carving: Blue Ribbon Techniques, by William Veasey and Cary Schuler Hull
Bills and Feet: An Artisan's Handbook, by William Veasey and Sina Kurman
Waterfowl Painting: Blue Ribbon Techniques, by William Veasey
Waterfowl Illustrated, by Tricia Veasey

Coming books

Blue Ribbon Burning Techniques, by William Veasey

Library of Congress Catalog Number: 84—51189.

Printed in the United States of America.
ISBN: 0-88740-023-X
Published by Schiffer Publishing Limited, Box E, Exton, Pennsylvania 19341

This book may be purchased from the publisher.
Please include $1.50 postage.
Try your bookstore first.

Introduction

The winning of the World Class at the Ward Foundation World Championship Carving Competition is to the wildfowl carver the most valued prize today. The competition began in 1971. The winning carving in the World Class that year, being one of the forerunners of decorative decoy carvings, was untextured and not unlike the working decoy. Today, the winning carvings of the World Class are barely discernable from the real birds. What has until very recently been termed a craft is just now being recognised as a fine art.

This book is designed in part as an acknowledgement and salute to the carvers of the past and present. The commitment that these carvers have shown in their work is responsible for the transformation from craft to art. In the last few years it has been evident that there is a desire and need for a photographic recording of the most acclaimed carvings each year. It is said that decorative decoy carving is the only art form/craft native to America. Given that, it would be a great loss to the history of art were the carvings of this important period to go unrecorded.

Each year, for three days, the finest carvings from around the world come together in one place. Because those carvings will never all be together again, Tom Johnson and I took on the project of chronicling the event. This book includes photos of 1984's World Class winners, most professional blue ribbon winners, as well as many amateur and novice blue ribbon winners. It contains many second place carvings as well as others. A special section is devoted to photographs of the past Best In World carvings. Biographical information is provided about most of the carvers whose birds are pictured herein.

Possibly the most important function of this book is to provide a compilation of the very carvings one goes to the show to study. It has been my observation that many carvers attend shows in order to learn. This can be used as a new tool to the further refinement of wildfowl carving. We learn from one another.

Dedication

This poem, written by Tan Brunet, most poignantly expresses the sentiments of the authors. Along with Tan, we dedicate this book to all those who support the growth and continuance of the Ward Foundation and the World Championships.

The World of '84

The morn was misty,
Cool and hazy —
Loon at bay,
Fishing lazy.

A cup of coffee,
In the quiet early dawn.
A final reminder
Of the excitement before the Storm.

Now the time is come
It's been a year since then —
Same old tune says he,
"Couldn't finish
Ran out of time again".

But all is well
And friends arrive;
With birds of song,
Decoys and owls.

Me, I'm happy
Just being here —
No, I'm not going to be the champ,
At least, not this year.

This Art is ours
And proud be our score,
The greatest of all artists
Come to compete on the shore.

They come from a-far
A-close and a-way
With smiles or gripes
They come anyway.

Hey boys! Look there's J.B.
Listen to the wisdom —
And quiet you be.
I'm here to compete,
Says he with a grin
But best of all —
I get to see all the guys again.

Amateurs and collectors,
Novice and pro;
They come for their joy,
All in a row.

The words of Big John,
To the young he said,
"Although you didn't win,
They know that you're in
You gotta get mad
And hit them again".

'84 was exciting,
But not many tears
But Listen...
Did I hear someone say,
"Wait till next year".

Table of Contents

THE WARD FOUNDATION

"Dedicated to wildfowl carving and painting, and to the historical, educational and environmental aspects of this art form". What better way to honor two of the worlds most famous carvers, Lem and Steve Ward of Crisfield, Maryland, than to choose their name for a foundation that would soon be the byword of the carving world.

1968 was the year that a group of business men, dedicated local DelMarVa carvers and hunters got together and decided that a central place was needed to properly exhibit this art form called "Decorative Bird Carving" — not an old antique hunting decoy but a true to life "Mantle" bird.

An exhibition was held that year and future plans called for not only showing the birds but to actually have a competition to find out who was the "best". In 1971 the first carving competition began which soon led to the annual Ward Foundation World Championship Wildfowl Carving Competition, now held each spring in Ocean City, Maryland. Now, thousands of birds line the tables and hundreds of waterfowl are floated in the tanks as champions, old and new vie for the coveted "Ward Foundation Blue Ribbon".

The exhibition of the winning birds and many others now takes place each fall in October at the Wicomico County Youth and Civic Center in Salisbury, Maryland.

Also in the same city may be found the North American Wildfowl Art Museum of the Ward Foundation located on the campus of Salisbury State College. Established in 1974 with volunteers and the renovation of an old dining hall, the museum was to become the largest of its kind in the United States. Today it has a 23,000 piece collection, its own quarterly magazine and a paid museum director and staff.

What does the future hold? Already there is a branch museum facility at Crisfield, Maryland, almost as large as the one in Salisbury. The contest will grow, the entries more numerous and this will continue to be the unique and only true art form of North America.

Canada Goose — Ward Brothers *(Courtesy of the Ward Foundation)*

Acknowledgments

We would like to thank many people for making a difficult task less arduous.
We appreciate all the support Knute Bartrug has given us throughout this project.
Thank you to Julie Mosher and Carol Dyke, at the office of the Ward Foundation for supporting the photographing of the past winners and for the prompt handling of other necessary details.
Thank you also to Ken Basil at the Ward Foundation Museum.
We'd like to acknowledge the Ocean City Convention Hall and its director, Gary Fisher, for facilitating us in the process of photographing.
We especially appreciate the aid that friendship brought from Dotty Veasey, William Rabjohns, and Terry Hand.
Thank you Curt Fabre for rounding up a few lost Louisianans.
And speaking of Louisianans, thank you Tan Brunet for contributing your 1984 competition-inspired poem.
We'd like to acknowledge the Ward Foundation for existing.
Thank you finally, and most importantly, to all the carvers, not only for sharing their success and their works with us, but also for their commitment to excellence.

Ward miniatures *(From the collection of Dr. Kramer)*

World Class

World Class Decorative Lifesize

Bob White Quail, titled "Needles, feathers and bone", by Ernie Muehlmatt won Best in World 1984 World Class Lifesize decorative *(Tom Johnson)*

Gambril Quail, by A.J. Rudisill won Second in World 1984 WCDL. *(Tom Johnson)*

Spruce Grouse pair, by Grant Goltz won Third in World 1984 WCDL *(Tom Johnson)*

Grouse, by A.J. Rudisill won 3rd in World 1984 WCDL *(Tom Johnson)*

World Class floating Pairs

Wigeon pair, by Pat Godin won Best in World 1984 World Class Competition Grade Floating Waterfowl *(Tom Johnson)*

Godin, hen head *(Tricia Veasey)*

Godin, hen chest *(Tricia Veasey)*

Godin, close-up drakes head *(Tricia Veasey)*

Godin, hen wing part unfolded *(Tricia Veasey)*

Godin, hen shoulder area, note wing tucked under side feathers *(Tricia Veasey)*

Godin, drake back *(Tricia Veasey)*

Godin, drake side, tertials *(Tricia Veasey)*

Godin, drake side *(Tricia Veasey)*

Godin, drake tail *(Tricia Veasey)*

Godin, hen tail with primary tips *(Tricia Veasey)*

Godin, hen side *(Tricia Veasey)*

Wigeon pair, by John Gewerth won Second in World 1984 World class Competition Grade Floating Waterfowl *(Tom Johnson)*

Wigeon pair, by Dick Bonner won Third in World 1984 World Class Competition Grade Floating Waterfowl *(Tom Johnson)*

Awards presentation for winners of World Class Floating Waterfowl by Knute Bartrug to (left to right) Pat Godin, John Gewerth, and Dick Bonner *(Tricia Veasey)*

Awards Presentation for Floating Pairs

World Class Miniatures

Guge, close-up head *(Tricia Veasey)*

Guge, top view *(Tricia Veasey)*

Mourning Doves, by Robert Guge won Best in World 1984 World Class Decorative Miniature Wildfowl *(Tricia Veasey)*

Three turkeys, by Manfred K. Scheel won Second in World 1984 World Class Decorative Miniature Wildfowl *(Tricia Veasey)*

Scheel, close-up *(Tricia Veasey)*

Sage Grouse males, by J.E. Hazeley won Third in World 1984 World Class Decorative Miniature Wildfowl *(Tricia Veasey)*

Judging World Class Miniatures (Tricia Veasey)

World Class Heads

Mallard hen head, by George Kruth won first place 1984 World Championship Waterfowl Head Contest *(Tricia Veasey)*

Ruddy Duck drake head, by Joy Yax won second place 1984 World Championship Waterfowl Head Contest *(Tricia Veasey)*

Shoveler drake head, by George Kruth won third place 1984 World Championship Waterfowl Head Contest *(Tricia Veasey)*

World Class Feather

Lady Amhearst feather, by Jim Sherman won first place 1984 World Championship Feather Contest *(Tricia Veasey)*

Judging World Class *(Tricia Veasey)*
Judging World Class Decorative Lifesize *(Tricia Veasey)*

Professional

Professional Decorative Lifesize

Bufflehead drake, by Harry Schneider won second place in professional decorative life-size waterfowl
(Tom Johnson)

Schneider, close-up head *(Tricia Veasey)*

Goslings, by Lynn Forehand won first place in professional decorative life-size waterfowl *(Tom Johnson)*

Schncider, upper wing detail *(Tricia Veasey)*

Schneider, tail *(Tricia Veasey)*

Schneider, under wing *(Tricia Veasey)*

Wood Duck drake, by Tan Brunet won third place in professional decorative life-size waterfowl *(Tom Johnson)*

Willet, by John Scheeler won first place in professional decorative life-size shorebirds *(Tom Johnson)*

Scheeler, Willet underside *(Tom Johnson)*

John Scheeler Willet, first place and second in show 1984 *(Tom Johnson)*

Clapper Rail, by John Scheeler won second place in professional decorative life-size shorebirds *(Tom Johnson)*

Clapper Rail, by W. Barton Walter won third place in professional decorative life-size shorebirds *(Tom Johnson)*

Spruce grouse, by Ernie Muehlmatt won first place in professional decorative life-size upland game *(Tom Johnson)*

Screech Owl, by Larry Barth won first place professional decorative life-size birds of prey *(Tom Johnson)*

Top left:
Barth, back view Screech Owl, first place and first in show *(Tom Johnson)*

Bottom left:
Kestrel, by Robert Guge won third place in professional decorative life-size birds of prey *(Tom Johnson)*

Sharp Shinned Hawk with Starling, by John Scheeler won second place in professional decorative life-size birds of prey *(Tom Johnson)*

Dove Kie, by Robert Ptashnik won first place in professional decorative life-size sea birds *(Tom Johnson)*

Tern, by John E. Dodge won second place in professional decorative lifesize seabirds *(Tom Johnson)*

White Throated Sparrow, by Ernie Muehlmatt won honerable mention *(Tricia Veasey)*

Tree Sparrow, by Robert Guge won first place in professional decorative life-size songbirds and first in show *(Tricia Veasey)*

ELTON
HENNING
1984

Woodpeckers, by Andrew Assimos won third place in professional decorative life-size stained or natural *(Tricia Veasey)*

Red Tailed Hawk, by Elton Henning won first place in professional decorative life-size stained or natural *(Tom Johnson)*

Judging for professional floating waterfowl *(Tricia Veasey)*

Left to right, third in show Cackling goose by Jack Bucko, best in show Mallard drake by Tan Brunet, second in show Eider hen by Sina Patricia Kurman *(Tricia Veasey)*

Professional Decorative Decoys

Mallard drake, by Tan Brunet won first in professional decorative decoy Mallards, first in division (Marsh Ducks) and first in show *(Tom Johnson)*

Brunet, Mallard in tank *(Tricia Veasey)*

Brunet, Mallard chest *(Tricia Veasey)*

Brunet, upper back *(Tricia Veasey)*

Brunet, side *(Tricia Veasey)*

Brunet, curl on tail *(Tricia Veasey)*

Brunet, different angle of side and back *(Tricia Veasey)*
Brunet, secondary, tertial area *(Tricia Veasey)*

Mallard hen, by Arnold Mummert won second place in professional decorative decoy Mallards *(Tricia Veasey)*

Mummert, chest *(Tricia Veasey)*

Mummert, head *(Tricia Veasey)*

Mummert, side *(Tricia Veasey)*

Mallard drake, by Bob Nagel won third place professional decorative decoy Mallards *(Tom Johnson)*

Above right:
Black Duck, by Jim Sprankle won first in professional decorative decoy Black Ducks *(Tricia Veasey)*

Below right:
Sprankle, head with foot *(Tricia Veasey)*

Black Duck, by Cap.'t Fred Muhs won second place in professional decorative decoy Black Ducks *(Tom Johnson)*

Black Duck, by Dan Cobb won third in professional decorative decoy Black Ducks *(Tom Johnson)*

Pintail drake, by Pat Godin won first in professional decorative decoy Pintails and second in division (Marsh Ducks) *(Tricia Veasey)*

Godin, close-up head *(Tricia Veasey)*

Godin, upper back and back of head *(Tricia Veasey)*

Godin, area of tertial coverts *(Tricia Veasey)*

Godin, rump area and primaries *(Tricia Veasey)*

Godin, tertials *(Tricia Veasey)*

Godin, side, where head joins back *(Tricia Veasey)*

Pintail drake, by Tan Brunet won second place in professional decorative decoy pintails *(Tricia Veasey)*

Brunet, close-up head *(Tricia Veasey)*

Brunet, tertial, primary, tail area *(Tricia Veasey)*

Green-Winged Teal Drake, by Timmy Zerangue won first in professional decorative decoy Green-Winged Teal *(Tricia Veasey)*

Green-Winged Teal hen by Dan Brown won second in professional decorative decoy Green-Winged Teal *(Tricia Veasey)*

Brown, head *(Tricia Veasey)*

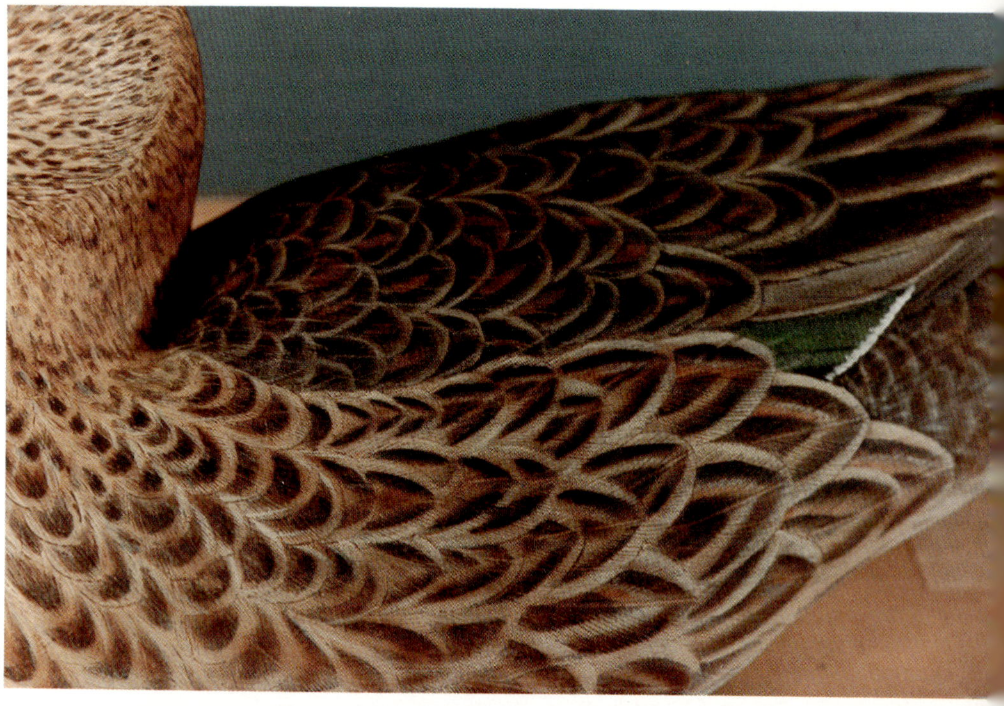

Brown, side *(Tricia Veasey)*

Brown, rump area *(Tricia Veasey)*

Green-Winged Teal hen, by Dan Cobb won third place in professional decorative decoy Green-Winged Teal *(Tricia Veasey)*

Wigeon hen, by Marc Shultz won first place in professional decorative decoy Wigeons *(Tricia Veasey)*

Shultz, close-up head *(Tricia Veasey)*

Wigeon hen, by Reagan Danos won third place in professional decorative decoy Wigeons *(Tricia Veasey)*

Wigeon drake, by Jett Brunet won second place in professional decorative decoy Wigeons *(Tricia Veasey)*

Cinnamon Teal drake, by Jim Sprankle won first in professional decorative decoy Cinnamon Teal *(Tom Johnson)*

Cinnamon Teal drake, by Don Brewer Jr. won second place in professional decorative decoy Cinnamon Teal *(Tom Johnson)*

Cinnamon Teal drake, by Ron Broadwater won third place in professional decorative decoy Cinnamon Teal *(Tricia Veasey)*

Wood Duck drake, by Mike Bonner won 2nd place in professional decorative decoy Wood Ducks *(Tom Johnson)*

Blue-Winged Teal drake, by Leo H. McIntosh Jr. won first place in professional decorative decoy Blue-Winged Teal *(Tricia Veasey)*

McIntosh, back *(Tricia Veasey)*

Blue-Winged Teal, by Bob Nagel won second place in professional decorative decoy Blue-Winged Teal *(Tricia Veasey)*

Nagel, head *(Tricia Veasey)*

Strauss, head *(Tricia Veasey)*

Blue-Winged Teal hen, by Tom Strauss won third place in professional decorative decoy Blue-Winged Teal *(Tricia Veasey)*

Gadwall drake, by Jim Sprankle won first in professional decorative decoy Gadwall *(Tricia Veasey)*

Gadwall drake by Thomas Birch won second place in professional decorative decoy Gadwall *(Tricia Veasey)*

Sprankle, close-up head *(Tricia Veasey)*

Sprankle, side detail *(Tricia Veasey)*

Sprankle, tertial covert area *(Tricia Veasey)*

Sprankle, side of chest *(Tricia Veasey)*

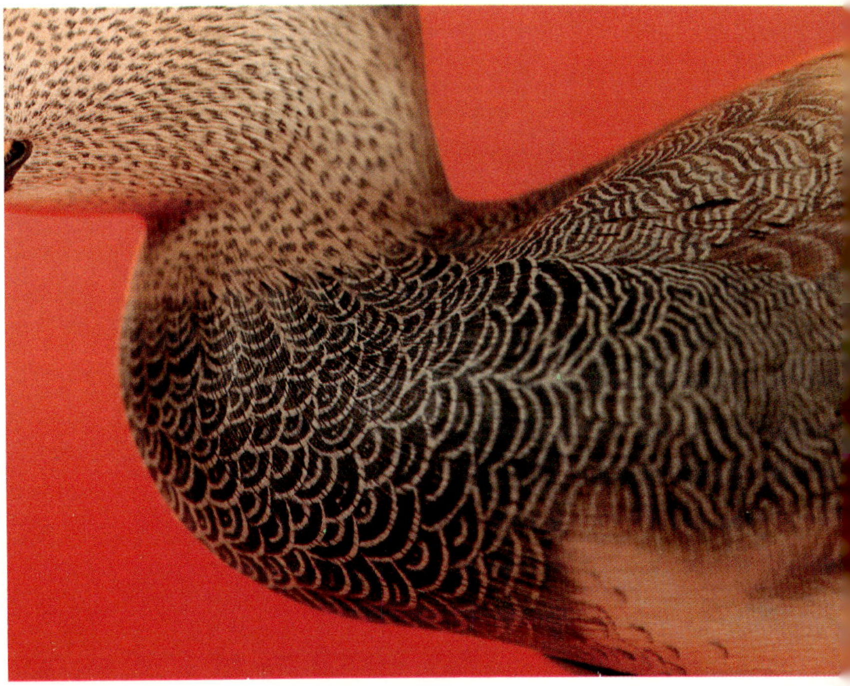

Gadwall drake, by Ray Eckert won third place in professional decorative decoy Gadwall *(Tricia Veasey)*

Shoveler drake, by Jim Sprankle won first place in professional decorative decoy Shovelers *(Tom Johnson)*

Sprankle, head *(Tricia Veasey)*

Sprankle, upper back *(Tricia Veasey)*

Sprankle, side (towards front of bird) *(Tricia Veasey)*

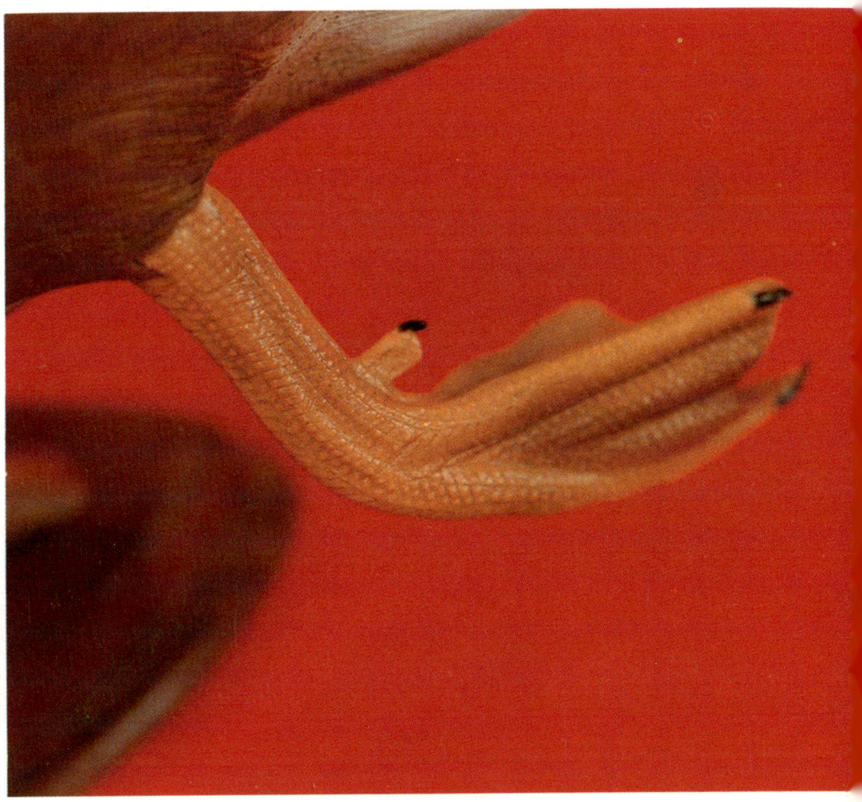

Sprankle, foot *(Tricia Veasey)*

Sprankle, other side (towards back of bird) *(Tricia Veasey)*

Shoveler hen, by Dan Cobb won third place in professional decorative decoy Shovelers *(Tom Johnson)*

Shoveler drake, by Mike Bonner won second place in professional decorative decoy Shovelers *(Tom Johnson)*

Canvasback hen, by Ken Scheeler won first place in professional decorative decoy Canvasbacks *(Tricia Veasey)*

Bufflehead hen, by Steve Collins won first place in professional decorative decoy Buffleheads *(Tricia Veasey)*

Scheeler, back *(Tricia Veasey)*

Scheeler, close-up head *(Tricia Veasey)*

Scheeler, chest *(Tricia Veasey)*

Scheeler, upper back *(Tricia Veasey)*

Scheeler, side (towards rump) *(Tricia Veasey)*

Barrow's Goldeneye drake, by Chris Bonner won first place in professional decorative decoy Goldeneyes *(Tricia Veasey)*

Bonner, close-up side *(Tricia Veasey)*

John G. Percy, close-up head *(Tricia Veasey)*

Goldeneye hen, by John G. Percy won second place in professional decorative decoy Goldeneyes *(Tricia Veasey)*

John G. Percy, chest *(Tricia Veasey)*

John G. Percy, side *(Tricia Veasey)*

Red-Breasted Merganser drake, by John Gewerth won first in professional decorative decoy Red-Breasted Mergansers and third in division (Divers) *(Tricia Veasey)*

Gewerth, side *(Tricia Veasey)*

Gewerth, close-up head *(Tricia Veasey)*

Gewerth, side of chest *(Tricia Veasey)*

Red-Breasted Merganser drake, by Pat Godin won second place in professional decorative decoy Red-Breasted Mergansers *(Tricia Veasey)*

Godin, close-up head *(Tricia Veasey)*

Godin, side of chest *(Tricia Veasey)*

Godin, side, towards front of bird *(Tricia Veasey)*

Godin, secondary/tertial area *(Tricia Veasey)*

Godin, tail *(Tricia Veasey)*

Hooded Merganser hen, by Habbart Dean won first place in professional decorative decoy Hooded Mergansers *(Tom Johnson)*

Dean, close-up head *(Tricia Veasey)*

Dean, close-up shoulder area *(Tricia Veasey)*

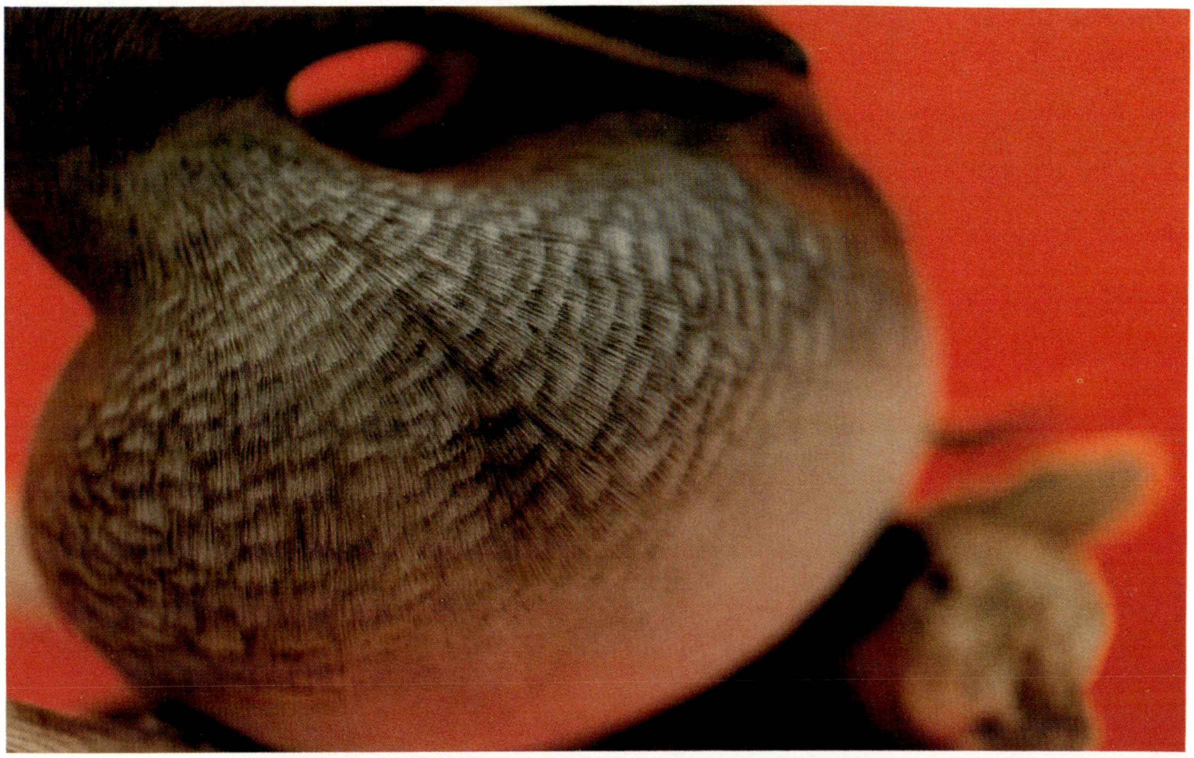

Dean, chest *(Tricia Veasey)*

Dean, tail and foot *(Tricia Veasey)*

Redhead drake, by Jett Brunet won first place in professional decorative decoy Redheads *(Tricia Veasey)*

Brunet, back and side *(Tricia Veasey)*

Ruddy Duck drake, by Tom Strauss won second place in professional decorative decoy Ruddy Ducks *(Tricia Veasey)*

Strauss, close-up head *(Tricia Veasey)*

Sprankle, close-up head *(Tricia Veasey)*

Ruddy Duck drake, by Jim Sprankle won first place in professional decorative decoy Ruddy Ducks *(Tricia Veasey)*

Scaup, by William Mueller won first place in professional decorative decoy Scaup *(Tricia Veasey)*

Ringneck drake, by Jim Sprankle won first place in professional decorative decoy Ringnecks *(Tricia Veasey)*

American Merganser drake, by Donald McKinlay won first place in professional decorative decoy American Mergansers *(Tom Johnson)*

Eider hen, by Sina Patricia Kurman won first place in professional decorative decoy Eiders and first place in division (Divers), and second in show *(Tom Johnson)*

Scoter, by Greg Ewell won first place in professional decorative decoy Scoters *(Tom Johnson)*

Old Squaw drake, by Ken Scheeler won first place in professional decorative decoy Old Squaws *(Tom Johnson)*

Old Squaw drake, by Tim Bourque won second place in professional decorative decoy Old Squaws *(Tricia Veasey)*

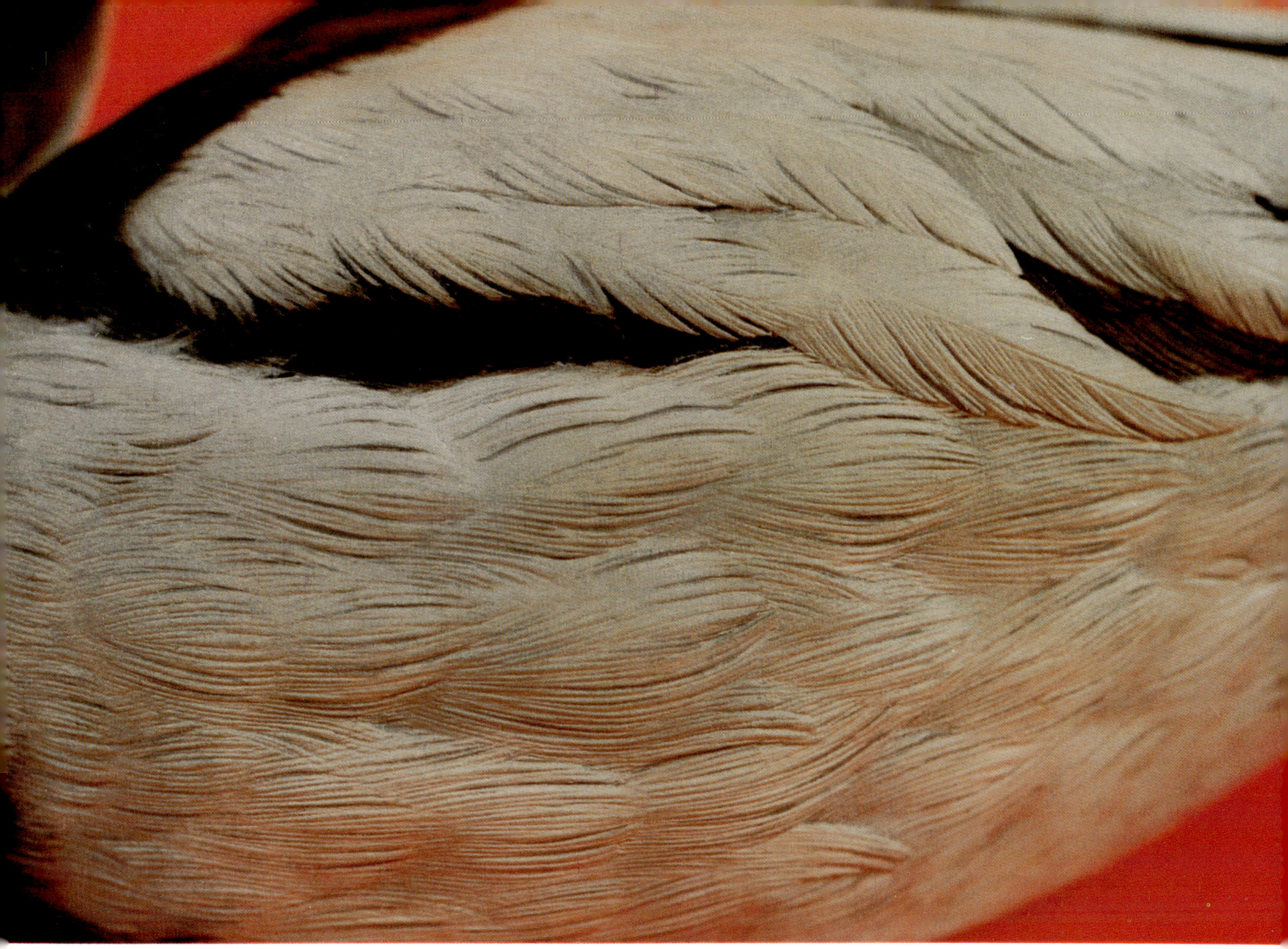

Bourque, close-up side *(Tricia Veasey)*

Bourque, head *(Tricia Veasey)*

Bourque, chest *(Tricia Veasey)*

Cackling Goose, by Jack Bucko won first place in professional decorative decoy goose and confidence decoys Canada Geese *(Tricia Veasey)*

Bucko, side and chest *(Tricia Veasey)*

Bucko, head *(Tricia Veasey)*

Bucko, upper back *(Tricia Veasey)*

Bucko, tertial/primary/tail area *(Tricia Veasey)*

Atlantic Brant, by June Noll won first place in professional decorative decoy geese and confidence decoys Brants *(Tricia Veasey)*

Blue Goose, by Len Carnaghi won first place in professional decorative decoy geese and confidence decoys, all other geese *(Tricia Veasey)*

Coot, by Reagan Danos won first place in professional decorative decoys geese and confidence decoys Coots and 3rd in division (confidence) *(Tricia Veasey)*

Grebe, by Joy Yax won first place in professional decorative decoy geese and confidence decoys Grebes *(Tricia Veasey)*

Grebe, by Donald Mckinlay won second place in professional decorative decoy geese and confidence decoys Grebes *(Tricia Veasey)*

Grebe, by Donald McKinlay won third place in professional decorative decoy geese and confidence decoys Grebes *(Tricia Veasey)*

Loon, by Jim Reynolds won first place in professional decorative decoy geese and confidence decoys Loons *(Tricia Veasey)*

Judging *(Tricia Veasey)*

Mandarin drake, by Harris J. Guidry Jr. won first place in professional decorative decoy geese and confidence decoys, all other confidence *(Tricia Veasey)*

Guidry, close-up head *(Tricia Veasey)*

Professional Decorative Miniatures

Green-Winged Teal drake, by William Rice won first place in professional decorative decoy miniatures waterfowl *(Tricia Veasey)*

Eider pair with decoy, by Keith A. Mueller won second place in professional decorative decoy miniature waterfowl *(Tricia Veasey)*

Hooded Merganser drake, by Jeff Butler won third place in professional decorative miniature waterfowl *(Tricia Veasey)*

Ruddy Turnstones, by Robert Guge won first place in professional decorative miniature shorebirds and second in show *(Tom Johnson)*

Woodcock, by Robert Ptashnik won honorable mention *(Tricia Veasey)*

Woodcock, by Carol Speegle won honorable mention *(Tricia Veasey)*

Pheasants, by Gary Yoder won first place in professional decorative miniature upland game, and third in show *(Tom Johnson)*

Barn Owl, by Lee Brown won first place in professional decorative miniature birds of prey *(Tricia Veasey)*

Loon, by Keith A. Mueller won first place in professional decorative miniature sea birds *(Tricia Veasey)*

Seagulls, by Keith Conrad won first place in professional decorative miniature stained or naturals *(Tricia Veasey)*

Chipping Sparrows, by Penny Miller won third place in professional decorative miniature songbirds *(Tricia Veasey)*

Cardinal pair, by Robert Guge won second place in professional decorative miniature songbirds *(Tricia Veasey)*

Amateur Decorative Lifesize

Wood Duck family, by J.E. Hazeley won first place in Amateur decorative life-size waterfowl and second in show *(Tricia Veasey)*

Judging decorative amateur class *(Tricia Veasey)*

Hooded Merganser drake, by J.E. Hazeley won second place in amateur decorative life-size waterfowl *(Tom Johnson)*

Sanderlings, by Jan Reese won first place in amateur decorative life-size shorebirds *(Tricia Veasey)*

California Quail, by J.E. Hazeley won first place in amateur decorative life-size upland game *(Tricia Veasey)*

Kestrel, by Willard E. Shantz won first place in amateur decorative life-size birds of prey *(Tricia Veasey)*

Pygmy Owl with Black Capped Chicadees, by Jim and Betty Cumming won second place in amateur decorative life-size birds of prey *(Tom Johnson)*

Loon, by Cliff Dunlap won first place in amateur decorative life-size sea birds and first in show *(Tom Johnson)*

Loon, by Burt Barker won second place in amateur decorative life-size sea birds *(Tom Johnson)*

Carolina Wren, by Edna Fenton won first place in amateur decorative life-size songbirds and third in show *(Tricia Veasey)*

Fenton, close-up head *(Tricia Veasey)*

Preening Bob White Quail, by Paige Paulson won first place in amateur decorative life-size stained or naturals *(Tricia Veasey)*

Amateur Decorative Decoys

Green-Winged Teal hen, by Curtis J. Fabre won first place in amateur decorative decoy marsh ducks, Green-Winged Teal *(Tom Johnson)*

Mallard drake, by Bert Cartwright won first place in amateur decorative decoy marsh ducks, mallards *(Tom Johnson)*

Pintail drake, by Eugene Morelli and Joan Zygmunt won first place in amateur decorative decoy marsh ducks, Pintails *(Tricia Veasey)*

Morelli and Zygmunt, rump area *(Tricia Veasey)*

Morelli and Zygmunt, close-up back/side *(Tricia Veasey)*

Blue-Winged Teal drake, by Dick Ledford won first place in amatuer decorative decoy marsh ducks, Blue-Winged Teal *(Tom Johnson)*

Cinnamon Teal, by Robert C. Jameison won first place in amateur decorative decoy marsh ducks, Cinnamon Teal *(Tom Johnson)*

Gadwall drake, by Russell Martin Jr. won first place in amateur decorative decoy marsh ducks, Gadwalls and first in division (marsh ducks) *(Tom Johnson)*

Hooded Merganser drake, by Tom Webb won first place in amateur decorative decoy diving ducks and second in division (divers) *(Tricia Veasey)*

Redhead drake, by Scat Pitre won first place in amateur decorative decoy diving ducks, Redheads *(Tricia Veasey)*

Ruddy Duck hen, by Bert Cartwright won first place in amateur decorative decoy diving ducks, Ruddy Ducks *(Tom Johnson)*

Ringneck drake, by Erwin Pillsbury won first place in amateur decorative decoy diving ducks, Ringnecks *(Tom Johnson)*

Canada Goose, by Robert Sakuta won first place in amateur decorative decoy geese and confidence decoys and first in division (geese) and second in show *(Tom Johnson)*

Emperor Goose, by L.R. Aukerman won first place in amateur decorative decoy geese and confidence decoys and third in division (all other geese) *(Tricia Veasey)*

Grebe, by D.J. Fasking won second place in amateur decorative decoy geese and confidence decoys, grebes *(Tricia Veasey)*

Loon, by Frank Ryan won first place in amateur decorative decoy geese and confidence decoys, loons *(Tom Johnson)*

Common Tern, by Jim Sherman won first place in amateur decorative decoy geese and confidence decoys, all other confidence and second in division (geese and confidence) *(Tricia Veasey)*

Cormorant, by Penelope Mace won second place in amateur decorative decoy geese and confidence decoys, all other confidence *(Tricia Veasey)*

Amateur Decorative Miniatures

Pintail drake, by Herb Watson won first place in amateur decorative miniature waterfowl *(Tricia Veasey)*

Whimbrel, by Terry Buckwalter won first place in amateur decorative miniature shorebirds *(Tricia Veasey)*

Grouse, by Ron Kagarise won first place in amateur decorative miniature upland game *(Tricia Veasey)*

Kestrel, by Ron Kagarise won first place in amateur decorative miniature birds of prey and second in show *(Tricia Veasey)*

Loon, by Wendy Michael won first place in amateur decorative miniature sea birds and third in show *(Tricia Veasey)*

Canvasback pair, by Virginia "Betsy" Cameron won first place in amateur decorative miniature stained or naturals *(Tricia Veasey)*

Brown Thrasher, by Jim Sherman won first place in amateur decorativ decoy miniature songbirds and first in show *(Tricia Veasey)*

Sherman, close-up *(Tricia Veasey)*

Judging *(Tricia Veasey)*

Mallard drake, by John D. Personette won first place in novice decorative marsh ducks, mallards *(Tricia Veasey)*

Novice Carvers

Black duck, by Jeff Muhs won first place in novice decorative marsh ducks, Blackducks and second in division (marsh ducks) *(Tricia Veasey)*

Green-Winged Teal hen, by Jack Walker won first place in novice decorative marsh ducks, Green-Winged Teal *(Tricia Veasey)*

Wood Duck drake, by Carol Kinney won first place in novice decorative marsh ducks, Wood Ducks *(Tricia Veasey)*

Blue-Winged Teal drake, by Bob Manning won first place in novice decorative marsh ducks, Blue-Winged Teal *(Tricia Veasey)*

Gadwall drake, by E.J. Hamm won first place in novice decorative marsh ducks, Gadwall *(Tricia Veasey)*

Shoveler drake, by Bob Downs won first place in novice decorative marsh ducks *(Tricia Veasey)*

Bufflehead drake, by Jim B. Ganley won first place in novice decorative diving ducks, Buffleheads *(Tricia Veasey)*

Canvasback hen, by E.R. Michalik won first place in novice decorative diving ducks, Canvasbacks *(Tricia Veasey)*

American Goldeneye drake, by Janet Someroff won first place in novice decorative diving ducks, Goldeneyes *(Tricia Veasey)*

Redhead drake, by Troy Danos won first place in novice decorative diving ducks, redheads and third in division (divers) *(Tricia Veasey)*

Hooded Merganser drake, by Paul Doherty won first place in novice decorative diving ducks, Hooded Mergansers *(Tricia Veasey)*

American Merganser drake, by L.E. Watkins won first place in novice decorative diving ducks, American Mergansers *(Tricia Veasey)*

Scaup, by W.J. Mick Brazell won first place in novice decorative diving ducks, Scaup and second in division (divers) *(Tricia Veasey)*

Scoter, by George Agardi, II. won first place in novice decorative diving ducks, Scoters *(Tricia Veasey)*

American Eider drake, by John P. English won first place in novice decorative diving ducks, Eiders *(Tricia Veasey)*

Old Squaw drake, by Betsy Piper won first place in novice decorative diving ducks, Old Squaws *(Tricia Veasey)*

Canada Goose, by Betsy Piper won first place in novice decorative geese and confidence decoys, Geese and second in division (geese) *(Tricia Veasey)*

Brant, by Anthony Christofich won first in novice decorative geese and confidence, Brant and third in division (confidence) *(Tricia Veasey)*

Coot, by Hamilton Dantin won first in novice decorative geese and confidence decoys, coots *(Tricia Veasey)*

Ruddy Duck drake, by Dale R. Dinse won first place in novice decorative diving ducks, Ruddy Ducks and first in division (divers) *(Tricia Veasey)*

Dove pair, by Eldridge Arnold was entered in the World Class Decorative Life-size Wildfowl competition *(Tricia Veasey)*

Lem and Steve Ward "Shootin Stool"

Lem and Steve Ward "Shootin Stool" working decoy winners; first place Canvasback hen by Paul Dobrosky, second place Brant by Terry McNulty, third place Red-Breasted Merganser by Keith A. Mueller *(Tricia Veasey)*

Lem and Steve Ward "Shootin Stool" silent auction donation winners; first place Chipping Sparrow by Penny Miller, second place Ruddy Turnstone by Robert Guge, third place Chickadee by Ernie Muehlmatt *(Tricia Veasey)*

Past Winners of the

"This is *to me* Lemuel T. Ward Jr. Born September 19th 1896 The best, most natural counterfeit my hands has ever accomplished of the Canada Goose" L.T. Ward 1965 *(Tricia Veasey)*

Old Squaw pair, by Jules Iski won Best in Show 1971 World Class Decorative Lifesize Waterfowl *(Tricia Veasey)*

"World" 1971-1983

Blue-Winged Teal, by J.B. Garton won Best in World 1971 World Class Decorative Decoy Pair *(Tricia Veasey)*

Mergansers, by John Scheeler won Best in Show 1972 World Class Decorative Decoy Pair *(Tricia Veasey)*, American Kestrels by John Scheeler won Best in World 1972 World Class Decorative Lifesize *(no photo available)*

Gadwalls by Jim Foote won Best in World 1973 World Class Decorative Decoy Pair *(Tricia Veasey)*, Perigrine Falcon with Green-Winged Teal by John Scheeler won Best in World 1973 World Class Decorative Lifesize *(no photo available)*

Redheads by Paul Burdette won Best in World 1974 World Class Decorative Decoy Pair *(Tricia Veasey)*

John Scheeler with carving 1975 *(Photograph compliments of Ward Foundation)*

Prairie Falcon with Dove by John Scheeler won Best in World 1975 World Class Decorative Lifesize *(Photograph compliments Ward Foundation)*

Wigeons by Jim Foote won Best in World 1975 World Class Decorative Decoy Pair *(Tricia Veasey)*

Long Eared Owl with Mouse by John Scheeler won Best in World 1976 World Class Decorative Lifesize *(Photograph compliments Ward Foundation)*

Goldeneyes by Pat Godin won Best in World 1976 World Class Decorative Decoy Pair *(Tricia Veasey)*

Pintails by Tan Brunet won Best in World 1977 World Class Decorative Decoy Pair *(Tricia Veasey)*

Clapper Rails with Snail by A.J. Rudisill won Best in World 1978 World Class Decorative Lifesize *(Photograph compliments Ward Foundation)*

Buffleheads by Randy Tull won Best in World 1979 World Class Decorative Decoy Pair *(Tricia Veasey)*

Mallards by Tan Brunet won Best in World 1978 World Class Decorative Decoy Pair *(Tricia Veasey)*

Red Jungle Fowl by Lynn Forehand won Best in World 1979 World Class Decorative Lifesize *(Photograph compliments Ward Foundation)*

Woodcocks by Ernie Muehlmatt won Best in World 1979 World Class Decorative Miniatures *(Tricia Veasey)*

Black Ducks by Pat Godin won Best in World 1980 World Class Decorative Decoy Pair *(Tricia Veasey)*

Ruffed Grouse by John Scheeler won Best in World 1980 World Class Decorative Lifesize *(Photograph compliments Ward Foundation)*

Professional

Carvers Biographies

ELDRIDGE ARNOLD — Professional

Mourning Doves courting	World Class entry

ANDREW ASSIMOS — Professional

Pileated Woodpeckers (lifesize-stained)	3rd
Flamingo-Miniature (stained)	2nd
Red Jungle Fowl (miniature stained)	Honorable Mention

Where to start and what to use is sometimes a question for the beginning carver. Andrew decided back in 1943 to use a pocket knife and wood from packing crates. As he developed a more active awareness of what bird carving was all about, he began serious carving in 1980. He attributes that to his contact with the Ward Foundation and their efforts to encourage this great art form.

Entering competitions came naturally and soon he was accepting blue ribbons. This year at the World competition he won a 2nd, 3rd, and honorable mention.

LARRY BARTH — Professional

Screech Owl	1st and 1st in Show

Larry won first place with his Screech Owl and First in Show for Decorative Lifesize Professional.

1979 was a landmark year for Larry Barth. He graduated from Carnagie-Mellon University with a BA in fine arts and design, and he won second in world in World Class Decorative Lifesize with his Great Horned Owls. His work has been exhibited in the bird art exhibition of the Leigh Yawkey Woodson Art Museum. He has competed with great success for nine years in the Ward Foundation Shows. In 1984 he taught a summer seminar for the Ward Foundation. Teaching has convinced Larry that people don't need to learn how to carve as much as they need to be taught how to know their subjects.

THOMAS BIRCH — Professional

Gadwall Drake	2nd
Eider Drake	2nd

DICK BONNER — Professional

Widgeon Pair	3rd in world pairs

Dick was a taxidermist in Rockford, Michigan when he decided to enter the 1963 National Decoy Show. His enthusiasm for carving grew when he found the judges had awarded a 2nd to his bird in the tank.

Talent abounds in the family, with his wife Joan oil painting on driftwood and two of his sons, Mike and Chris, also winners this year, becoming proffessional carvers.

Chris, Dick, and Mike Bonner

The call of the water soon beckoned to Dick and his family and after purchasing a 35 foot sailboat, they lived 8 years on it traveling down the Mississippi River to New Orleans.

He began more serious carving again in 1982 and won ribbons in the Cajun Hunters Festival, and New Orleans Waterfowl Carvers Show.

1984 was the first time at the World Championship for Dick and his family and winning 3rd in the World Widgeon Pairs proves that his motto - "Carve from live subjects if possible" paid off.

TIM BOURQUE — Professional

Old Squaw Drake	2nd
Coot	2nd

DON BREWER JR. — Professional

Cinnamon Teal	2nd
Shoveler	Honorable Mention

Forty ribbons in four years is an excellent start for any beginning carver and "Best in Show" (Int. class) at the PFDA contest in Sacramento, California in 1982 was enough to make Don want to carve birds for a living.

He was introduced to his career by Bill Pinches, a California legend as a bayman and carver, and says "No one has ever done me a bigger favor". Don's goal, like other great carvers, is to be the best there is, and to do everything he can to promote the art.

When not carving he also builds sneakboats and scullboats for local hunters.

Maintaining an aviary is a carvers best resource and working from live birds make Don's carvings a much sought after art form.

Words of wisdom: If you want to be a professional carver, you'd better be serious about it. There are a lot of carvers out there trying to be better than you. It takes study, dedication and hard work.

RON BROADWATER Professional

Cinnamon Teal Drake	2nd
Goldeneye Drake	3rd
Shoveler Drake	Honorable Mention

Ron Broadwater is a native Marylander. His appreciation of wildlife and the outdoors began in his younger years while hunting and fishing with his father. As the years progressed the beauty and grace of wildfowl increasingly intriqued him and enhanced his desires to recreate these magnificant birds in wood.

In 1980, Ron started to give carving and painting as much attention as was available and thus began his drive to develop a new career. In the summer of 1983, Ron resigned as a Purchasing Manager and turned professional on a full-time basis.

Ron has achieved repeated success and won numerous ribbons and awards in "World" and other competitions. This success and his future potential accomplishments have made his works of art highly prized and sought after.

The love and lore of wildfowl, coupled with increasing knowledge and now a full-time dedication is easily reflected in his sculptures.

Words of Wisdom: "Study and Practice".

DAN BROWN Professional

Green-Winged Teal Hen	2nd

Dan is from Hebron, Maryland.

LEE BROWN Professional

Barn Owl (Miniature)	1st
Mourning Dove (Miniature)	2nd

Lee Brown has always had a strong interest in wildlife and has been carving birds since 1975. He pays great attention to detail and spends many hours of research on a species prior to its creation.

He enjoys working in both lifesize and miniature and competes annually in both the U.S. Nationals and the Ward Foundation World Championship. He has won many awards, including a "Best-in-Show" at the 1983 U.S. Nationals. Lee feels that competing is very beneficial since it encourages the carver to consistently improve. Lee's goal is to someday produce a "Best-in World" carving.

Lee exhibits at various Massachusetts Bird Carving shows and had a one-man exhibit at the Peabody Museum in Salem, MA. during the summer of 1983. He lives in Wakefield, MA. with his wife and three children.

Words of wisdom: Scrutinize each completed piece for areas of improvement and strive to make the next one better.

JETT BRUNET Professional

Redhead	1st
Widgeon	2nd

Following in your fathers footsteps and fame might be tough for some young men, but 19 year old Jett is a winner in his own right. He started traveling with his father, Tan Brunet, to all the local waterfowl shows when he was 10 years old. This exposed him to the world's greatest carvers, and he soon decided that he would some day compete against them.

1983 was the year Jett turned professional after receiving two "Best Teenage Carver Awards" in prior years. Blue ribbons, best-in-shows, and Best Amateur Carver in the World helped boost him into the professional class.

Words of wisdom: Jett's formula for a winning bird is: Get some good wood. Find plenty of reference on the bird, stay simple and don't rush. *Slow down.*

Tan and Jett Brunet

TAN BRUNET Professional

Cajun carver, poet, emotional award winner, teacher, judge and family man are among many words that describe Tan. The title "World Champion Decorative Decoy Pairs Carver" has been bestowed upon him many times also.

For the record: Pintails 1977, Mallards 1978, Canvasbacks 1981, Green Winged Teal 1982, and last year Redheads 1983. He is also a flatwork artist and prints are issued in a limited edition. Ask him a question about carving and you will come away a better carver.

Words of Wisdom: Use all research material available. Work from live birds when possible. Use full color mounts for proper colors. Get advice from the better carvers.

JACK BUCKO Professional

Cackling Goose	1st

Jack is from Merrillville, Indiana.

JEFF BUTLER Professional

Miniature Hooded Merganser Drake3rd

Jeff is from Hubbardstown, Massachusetts.

LEN CARNAGHI Professional

Blue Goose	1st

Len, world class carver, and probably best noted for his decorative carvings of geese, has been carving birds for over 20 years. Winner of well over 100 blue ribbons, his birds are sought after by many collectors.

His love for the outdoors, and careful study of the live bird, shows in the fine detail of his finished piece.

Len is also a collector of antique decoys and his collection of Ben Schmidt birds is one of the finest in North America.

His wife Marylin with their five children often accompany him to many shows.

Words of wisdom: Study your reference material before you start your carving.

DAN COBB Professional

Green-Winged Teal Hen	3rd

Dan is from Fairton, New Jersey.

STEPHEN E. COLLINS-The Birdman Professional

Bufflehead hen	1st

Pheasants by Gary Yoder won Best in World 1980 World Class Decorative Miniatures *(Tricia Veasey)*

Goshawk and Crow by John Scheeler won Best in World 1981 World Class Decorative Lifesize *(Photograph compliments Ward Foundation)*

Canvasbacks by Tan Brunet won Best in World 1981 World Class Decorative Decoy Pair *(Tricia Veasey)*

Least Bittern by Ernie Muehlmatt won Best in World 1981 World Class Decorative Miniatures *(Tricia Veasey)*

Stephen acknowledges Jon Jones for being the driving force behind his success and that of many other beginners.

He says it is important for beginners not to be afraid to compete.

Stephen is 35 years old and has been carving birds for about two years. He's worked with his hands on many other projects before carving. He's very much into sharing about birds, kids, hot rods, war stories, travel and model cars.

Words of Wisdom: Stephen's advice to beginners is not to get discouraged with their first carvings, just keep going.

KEITH CONRAD — Professional

Gulls of Walnut (stained)	1st

Keith has been carving for 3 years and lists blue ribbons at the York, PA show and a previous honorable mention at the World Wildfowl contest in 1983. He carves both natural finish and painted birds.

Words of wisdom: Study your work well. Take your time and go easy with the buring pen. Don't paint too heavily.

REAGAN DANOS — Professional

Widgeon Hen	3rd
Bufflehead Drake	3rd
Coot	1st & 3rd place confidence

Five years of carving, with over 200 awards is quite an accomplishment for 26 year old Reagan. He doesn't want to stop there. His goal is to be as great a carver as Tan Brunet, Jimmie Vizier, Pat Godin and others.

He continues to learn by going to the competitions, asking questions, and studying birds.

Words of wisdom: Don't give up. Everyone has a goal they want to meet, so keep trying.

HABBART DEAN — Professional

Hooded Merganser Hen	1st
Bufflehead	Honorable Mention

Habbart was born in Cambridge, Maryland, in the heart of the Chesapeake Bay area. His interest in waterfowl would naturally turn him to carving birds he knew best. Starting with primitive "stick types" in 1978 and then on to lifesize decoratives in 1980, brought him his first award in competition. As a novice that year he earned his first "best-in-show".

Since then, "open" competition at the World Championship, National Decoy Contest, and others have earned him many "blue" and "best-of-shows" numbering over 50.

Habbart is a member of the Advisory Board of the Ward Foundation and regulary exhibits at the annual fall show and other exhibitions on the east coast.

He also does work for reproduction, in various mediums which are marketed throughout the US and Canada. Habbart now devotes full time to carving, usually by commission.

PAUL DOBROSKY — Professional

Canvasback Working Decoy	1st

Paul is from Shrewsbury, New Jersey. He won the trophy and rosette this year for taking first place with his Canvasback in the Lem and Steve Ward "Shootin' Stool" competition.

JOHN E. DODGE — Professional

Tern with Fish	3rd

Making hunting decoys back in 1939 so he could hunt with his father, started John on his way to carving and competition. It was 1976 before he would begin decorative bird carving. Nearly 100 ribbons now have been awarded to John's birds.

Although he admits to never keeping records, John answers one of the questions asked most by the non-carver, "How long does it take to complete a decoy?", with an estimate of between 40 and 80 hours.

John feels his success in carving is the result of originality, realism and fine detailing. Working directly from photographs and mounted specimens helps avoid errors inherent in copy carving.

He exhibits his birds at many shows including the Ward Foundation Exhibition held annually in October and at the Clayton, N.Y. Wildlife Art Show each July.

RAY ECKERT — Professional

Gadwall Drake	3rd

Ray is from Fife Lake, Michigan.

GREG EWELL — Professional

Surf-Scoter	1st

Greg is an avid outdoorsman and his carvings of waterfowl show that he knows his birds. He has been carving for 8 years and recently became a professional, competing in shows across the U.S. and Canada.

Words of wisdom: Spend time studying the anatomy of the bird you are carving. Carve birds you know and enjoy.

LYNN FOREHAND — Professional

Goslings	1st

Lynn is a well known carver in the competition world. He is featured in the "Past Winners of the World" section of this book as well as the "Life Size Decorative" section for 1984. Lynn is from Chesapeake, Virginia.

JOHN GEWERTH — Professional

Widgeon Pairs	2nd in World
Red-Breasted Merganser Drake	1st & 3rd Best Diver

John has a goal that someday he would like to carve full time, but today he works as Manager of Organizational Development at Continental Can Company.

He began carving in 1975, mostly decorative floating decoys. He waited until 1977 to begin competing in open competition. John's awards have been many, including 10 Best-of-Shows, with one at the World Championship. He entered the Floating Decorative Decoy Pairs Competition at Ocean City in 1982 and 1984 and was awarded a Second Place Ribbon each time.

In the future, time permitting, John would like to create larger, more complex pieces.

Words of Wisdom: It has been an extremely satisfying experience for me. The keyword in any aspect of "nature's" art is "reference." Know your subject matter. This can be accomplished through many hours of study. If you're going to be a serious carver, this can't be shortchanged.

PAT GODIN — Professional

Wigeon Pair	Best in World
Pintail Drake	1st and 2nd Marsh Ducks
Red-Breasted Merganser	2nd

Words of Wisdom: In order for our creations to become recognized as true fine art and for us to be recognized as artists we must become less obsessed with technique and become more concerned with the basics of art such as design and color schemes as well as ideas and concepts. We should realize that to encourage such a healthy, progressive movement in the future, competitions must be judged more liberally to allow for artistic expression.

Pat Godin

GRANT E. GOLTZ Professional

Spruce Grouse	3rd in World - Lifesize

A casual entry in a decoy contest 10 years ago led Grant to a career in carving and many awards. He is a carver that likes to pay meticulous attention to detail as he considers the bird both a research and an art object. "To do a bird right, you have to know how they are put together, right down to the bone."

A goal set by Grant is to increase the public's appreciation of realism and accuracy in wildlife art.

Words of Wisdom: Before you do any bird, take the time to learn what goes where, and understand why. We have an obligation to ourselves, our fellow carvers and the art form to do better. If we can't accept this small responsiblity, we don't belong.

ROBERT GUGE Professional

Doves (Min.)	Best in World Decorative Miniature
Tree Sparrow	1st & 3rd in Show
Ruddy Turnstones (Min.)	1st & 2nd in Show
Kestrel	3rd
Cardinals (Min.)	2nd

Bob grew up in the Fox River Valley in Illinois, enjoying nature and bird watching. Twelve years ago he decided to apply that knowledge of birds to carving. He is a self taught artist with no formal training. He has been a full time carver for the past 5 years.

Bob has won many carving awards including the "Best of Show" at the Pacific Southwest Wildfowl Arts Show in February, 1983 and 1984; the International Decoy Contest in August, 1983; the U.S. Natinal Decoy Show in March, 1984 and numerous 1st Place Ribbons in the World Championship Wildfowl Carving Competitions in Ocean City, Maryland, including Best in World Decorative Miniature Class, 1984. His work is included in the permanent collection of the Leigh Yawkey Woodson Art Museum at Wausau, Wisconsin, the Wildfowl Art Museum, Salisbury, Maryland and in numerous private collections nationwide.

Words of Wisdom: I believe bird watching is one of the best ways you can help yourself in carving. Also start with simple carvings and learn your basics before tackling those big intricate pieces.

HARRIS "PECON" GUIDRY JR. Professional

Mandarin Duck	1st

Seven Best in Show awards and many Blue Ribbons have been awarded to the birds carved by "Pecon". He started carving in 1976 and as a Novice in the World Championship won his first ribbon, a Second Place.

He enjoys winning, but even more he likes the friends he has made while attending the shows.

Words of Wisdom: Be open-minded and listen to the experienced carvers. Profit from mistakes others have made. Attend shows and compare carvings.

ELTON HENNING Professional

Redtail Hawk	1st
Natural Wood	

Elton's method of carving is from the old school of chip carving, using knives and a V-gouge on his natural wood finished birds. After winning a First in 1983 with his Screech Owl and Mouse, he came back this year to take a Blue Ribbon with a Redtail Hawk.

Starting twenty years ago to carve gave him enough experience to begin full time carving as a career 12 years ago.

Elton was commissioned by General Motors to carve a Red-Tailed Hawk in flight for the cover of the 1984 Buick Book. He also has been invited to show at the Leigh Yawkey Woodson Art Museum in 1984.

GEORGE KRUTH Professional

Mallard Head	1st in world
Shoveler Head	3rd in world

Whittling around a campfire, and reading a top-notch carving book "Wildlife in Wood" by Richard LeMaster helped to develop George's skills and techniques.

As a first year carver in 1980 he won his first blue ribbon with an Upland Game bird at the Ward Foundation World Championship. He repeated in the open class at the Canadian National Decoy Contest in 1982. In 1983 he earned the Best Marsh Duck ribbon at the Canadian Show and 1st in the North American Decoy Carving Championships.

Words of wisdom: The basis for learning to carve is competition. Your attendance at the various competitions will introduce you to carvers, techniques, tools, and other references and aids. A judge's critique will give you direction and help to move you from plateau to plateau.

SINA PATRICIA KURMAN Professional

Eider Hen	1st in species-2nd in show

'Pat' attended Ohio State University and the Glassboro State Teacher's College in New Jersey. Her longtime interest in art led her to take lessons in decorative decoy carving in 1978, under the direction of William Veasey.

She has successfully competed in such shows as the United States Nationals in New York; Virginia Beach, Virginia; and the World Championship in Ocean City, Maryland. Her work has won numerous awards including Best of Shows.

Pat has taught decoy carving at the Academy of Natural Sciences in Philadelphia, Pennsylvania and is currently assisting Veasey in his seminars.

She has been invited to display the Eider hen at the Leigh Yawkey Woodson Art Museum.

"Along the Grand", Black Ducks and Muscrat by Pat Godin won Best in World 1982 World Class Decorative Lifesize *(Photograph compliments of the carver)*

Green-Winged Teal by Tan Brunet won Best in World 1982 World Class Decorative Decoy Pair *(Tricia Veasey)*

Mallards in Flight by Gary Yoder won Best in World 1982 World Class Decorative Miniatures *(Tricia Veasey)*

DONALD MCKINLAY — Professional

Grebe	2nd
American Merganser Drake	1st

LEO H. McINTOSH, JR. — Professional

Blue Winged Teal	1st
Green Winged Teal	Honorable Mention
Pintail	3rd

Leo has been a professional artist since high school, concentrating on canvas painting. He began working for an old-time decoy maker named Ken Harris and after 5 years had gained enough experience to branch out on his own. His decoys have since earned many ribbons.
Words of wisdom: Study live birds whenever possible, try to develop your own style. If you copy from other carvers you're always one step behind them. Inovate! Genius is one third inspiration and two thirds perspiration.

PENNY MILLER — Professional

Chipping Sparrow (Min.)	1st and Plaque
Pair Chipping Sparrows (Miniature)	3rd
Wood Thrush (Min.)	Honorable Mention

Penny carved her first piece - a Tufted Titmouse - in 1979. She is full-time carver and specializes in songbirds, both life size and miniature.

Penny is an enthusiastic bird watcher and the knowledge she has gained through this activity is reflected in her carvings. She believes that the most important part of her research is the observance of birds in nature and, for this reason, will rarely carve a bird which she has not studied in its natural environment.

Although Penny has been carving for a comparatively short period of time, she has won national recognition for her realistic songbirds. She has taken over eighty awards at major competitions and her carvings are in collections throughout the United States and several foreign countries. A carving of hers is included in the exhibit of the North American Wildfowl Art Museum of the Ward Foundation.
Words of Wisdom: Be fair with yourself. Many a beginning carver will compare their work with the best on the professional tables at competitions. This can be discouraging to a beginner. Give yourself a break and compare your work with people who have carved as long as you have been carving. Ask questions and don't be afraid to experiment.

BILL MUELLER — Professional

Bird	Place
Blue Bill Drake	1st place

Bill has been carving for about 7 years. In this time he has carved all of the divers that are common to his area. He has won 24 ribbons, 14 of which are blues and one Best in the diver division. Carving is a hobby for him and his goal is to continue carving every species known.

KEITH A. MUELLER — Professional

Common Eiders (Min.)	2nd
Common Loon (Min.)	1st
Ringneck Duck	3rd
Red-Breasted Merganser Shootin' Stool	3rd
Long Billed Curlew Shootin' Stool	Honorable Mention

Sea Ducks are Keith's specialty and his interest in them comes from being influenced by the "old masters". The decoy carvers of Connecticut, Maine and Nova Scotia from around the turn of the century have all been researched by him. The birds flying Long Island Sound are also his subjects as he duplicates them into working decoys.

He carves 200-250 birds a year, mostly for hunting, but still has the time to enter competition in the Decorative Class. Over 150 ribbons and 30 Best in Shows have been awarded to his birds.

His goal is to keep carving and be happy doing it.
Words of Wisdom: You have to pace yourself, realize what you are capable of carving at the time, and work with those skills. Do not carve what you are not familiar with. Research and learn your subjects. Carve one step at a time and have fun doing it. Take your time and always put your best effort into your work.

ERNIE MUEHLMATT — Professional

Quail (Bobwhite)	Best in the World Decorative Lifesize
Spruce Grouse	1st

A gift of hand-carved birds in 1967 led Ernie to a hobby which quickly became his career. Today he is recognized for his talent and ability, as well as uniqueness of style. At competitions such as the Long Island National Championship, The California Open, and the World Championship he has attained many Blue Ribbons, including 10 Best-in-Show.

His pair of miniature Woodcock made him World Champion in 1979. Again in 1981 he was World Champion with a pair of miniature Least Bittern.

This year, 1984, the Grand Prize was his when he won Best in the World, Lifesize Decorative. He has named it, appropriately, "Needles, Feathers and Bone."

Ernie's carvings are in many private collections and have been displayed at all the prominent shows on the east coast. His carvings are also on permanent display at the Ward Wildfowl Art Museum and Denver Museum.

CAPT. FRED MUHS — Professional

Black Duck — 2nd
Red-Breasted Merganser Hen — 3rd

Fred has won Blue Ribbons in all the major competitions on the east coast. He has been carving for 18 years and now carves full time at his own gallery on Long Island's South Shore.

Realism in the art of carving is what Fred is striving for. His birds are in collections thoughout the world.

Words of Wisdom: The basis for a good carving is research. Most important is your pattern. It's like building a house. If your foundation is correct, everything else should follow in its place.

ARNOLD MUMMERT — Professional

Mallard Hen — 2nd (1983)
Canvasback Hen — 2nd (1982)

Arnold carves only as a hobby making two or three birds a year. He started carving eight years ago and has taken classes with Bob Baile and Larry Hayden.

Words of Wisdom: "Find an experienced carver and enroll in classes available. Obtain and study pictures and skins — get to know the ducks. Attend shows and contests to see what can be done and talk with the vendors about their tools."

BOB NAGEL — Professional

Blue Wing Teal Drake — 2nd
Mallard Drake — 3rd

Bob won his first Blue Ribbon at the Ward Foundation World Championship in 1978. He has continued to carve and enter competitions ever since.

Bob's idea is to think big, but carve small, to learn techniques better.

JUNE NOLL — Professional

Brant — 1st

Combining a college major of art history and studio art with a lifelong study of nature and its relationship to color and texture led June to carve birds.

The many ribbons June has won in National competitions attest to her artistic ability. The Long Island Shore Bird Classic, the National Decoy Show, and the "World" contest have all awared her birds ribbons.

Words of wisdom: The biggest stumbling block that I find with my students is that they lack knowledge and reference material for their carving. The best advice I can give is to study that bird! Especially in the wild (live).

JOHN GORDON PERCY — Professional
Common Goldeneye — 2nd

Words of Wisdom: Be innovative. Use good reference material and plan well. Above all keep at it, a few minutes a night is better than leaving it for extended periods of time.

BETSY PIPER

Canada Goose — 1st & 2nd in Geese and Confidence
Ringneck Duck — 1st
Old Squaw — 1st
Lessor Scaup — 2nd

Betsy has been carving a little over 3 years and at the present time is the only woman carver in the Grosse Pointe Artists Association. She entered her first show in September, 1983 at Pointe Moiullee and won a 3rd Place award. In Atlanta, Georgia in April, 1984, she won many Blue Ribbons and 2 Best in Show.

Betsy takes lessons once a week from Joy Yax and would spend every minute of her life carving if it were possible. She shows her birds twice a year in June and September at the Grosse Pointe Artists Association Art Show, and every other year at the Junior League Show House.

Words of Wisdom: Good instructor, good references, pictures, birds or mounts.

ROBERT PTASHNIK — Professional

Dovekie — 1st
Woodcock (Min.) — Honorable Mention
Shootin' Stool — Honorable Mention

Born in Hanover, Ontario, Canada, Bob grew up fully appreciating the abundant wildlife in the area.

He came to the World Championship in 1975 with one bird. It won Best in Show, Amateur Class. He continued to enter competitions as a professional and has been awarded 19 Best in Show and many Blue Ribbons.

Bob was honored to be invited to show his work in England where one of his birds was presented to the Duchess of Devonshire.

The friendship of fellow artists and the many people he meets who share his love of birds makes his work truly a joy.

JIM REYNOLDS — Professional

Loon — 1st

Jim is a former school teacher and coach. He is a native of Michigan and the outdoors have been a very large part of his life. he hunts in the fall and had developed an interest in making his own hunting rig. This resulted in his appreciation of waterfowl. He became interested in carving in 1979 and entered his first competition that year in California. He won a Best in Show there in novice class. He has been a consistant winner since. He enters four or five competitions annually and sells most of his carvings in Michigan. He's won first place in the last three World Championship competitions. He also makes custom knives.

Words of Wisdom: "Know your subject and keep your knife sharp!"

Black-Crowned Night Heron by A.J. Rudisill won Best in World 1983 World Class Decorative Lifesize
(Photograph compliments Ward Foundation)

Redheads by Tan Brunet won Best in World 1983 World Class Decorative Decoy Pair *(Tricia Veasey)*

Avocets by Robert Ptashnik won Best in World 1983 World Class Decorative Miniatures *(Tricia Veasey)*

BILL RICE Professional

Green-Winged Teal	1st

Bill started carving decoys and little gamebirds about eight years ago. He has always had an interest in nature and birds and feels carving is natural for him. He grew up observing nature in the marshes when other kids were spending time with cars. He loved woodworking and found blending this with his fascination with wild creatures made carving a real joy.

About four years ago he began entering carvings at the United States Nationals in New York and the World Championship in Maryland and became serious about them. He found the shows very powerful in motivating him in that they challenged him to work toward showing his best there. He has been a successful winner at both shows.

A.J. RUDISILL Professional

Gambril Quail	Second in World

A.J. Rudisill is another well known carver who has been successfull in competitions of the past as well as today. His work is featured in the "Past Winners of the World" section of this book. He is from Atlantic City, New Jersey.

MANFRED K. SCHEEL Professional

3 Turkeys (Min.)	2nd Best in World

Manfred Scheel, who resides in Quakertown, Pennsylvania, has been practicing his craft for about 15 years. His early love of nature, especially birds, combined with his skill as a woodworker, led him to the field of bird carving.

Throughout the years, he has won numerous awards in some of the world's finest carving shows - including:

...2nd in World Miniature - 1982-84
Ward Foundation World Championship
...Best in Miniature
Long Island Open
Best in Miniature
Mid-Atlantic Waterfowl Festival

One of his main goals is to continue to strive for more meticulous representation of each bird he carves.

KEN SCHEELER Professional

Canvasback Hen	1st
Old Squaw Drake	1st

Ken is from Vineland, New Jersey.

JOHN S. SCHEELER Professional

Willet	1st
Sharp Shinned Hawk and Starling	2nd
Clapper Rail	2nd

"Master Carver," "World Champion," "Artist," are just some of the words that are used to describe John Scheeler. Seven (7) times he has been in the winners circle as his name was announced as the New World Champion. In the past 14 years his other carvings have won many blue ribbons and best of show.

He likes to carve birds of prey and game birds using all the help he can get from photographs, books, and an acquired knowledge of studying the live birds. "Know your subject," is good advice from John and "Listen to advice from other carvers."

HARRY SCHNEIDER Professional

Bufflehead Drake	2nd

Harry's interest in carving began in 1975. After seeing a decoy purchased by a close friend, Harry developed the urge to carve.

Two and a half years later, self taught, and with much persuasion, Harry entered his first competitive show at the Ward Foundation's World Championship held at Winter's Place, Salisbury, Maryland - 1978. Bringing home seven ribbons, one of which was a 1st place Blue - Novice Division, Harry became very encouraged. Entering each year thereafter, from Novice to Amateur, and now Professional, Harry took a 1st place Blue Ribbon in the Decorative Lifesize Waterfowl - Professional Division, 1982 World Championship at Ocean City, Maryland, with a Wood Duck. His "Woody Drake" also took 3rd in Show.

Born and raised in Baltimore and now residing in Lutherville, Maryland with his wife, LaVerne, carving has been most instrumental and rewarding.

MARCUS SCHULTZ Professional

Widgeon Hen	1st
Wood Duck Drake	1st

Following years of intimate familiarity with his father's (William L. Schultz) work, including many elaborate decorative pieces, Marc was finally motivated by, ironically, a pair of service Bluebills his father had just completed for a hunting decoy contest. Two years later Marc entered open competition and has won an average of three "Best of Shows" each year. Marc's work has been shown in the Leigh Yawkey Woodson Bird Art Exhibition each year since 1980.

Marc pursues a faithful rendering of his subject in his work. He strives first to capture the essential qualities of a species and feels detail must play a secondary role. He maintains, however, that details must be successfully done as a final proof of excellence. That combination of goals makes the rendering of birds in wood endlessly challenging.

Words of Wisdom: Marc repeately emphasizes three important areas to carvers that come for instruction:

Draw Your patterns - Become comfortable with form, anatomy and character in order to develop the confidence necessary when actually removing wood.

Observe - See when you look. Ask specific questions of yourself, then consult your source material for the answers.

Emphasize form - Don't get excited about detailing until you've established good, strong form.

CAROL R. SPEEGLE Professional

Woodcock (miniature)	Honorable Mention
Carolina Wren (miniature) natural	3rd

A magazine article in 1977 about the two master carvers, Grainger McKoy and Gilbert Maggioni, started Carol on her career of full time carving. Winning her first ribbon at the C.N.E. and learning from all the carvings prompted her to enter the Ward Foundation World Championship Contest where she has been a consistant winner. In 1979 Carol entered the U.S. Air Force and continued to carve in her spare time. She completed her enlistment in 1983 and began full time carving.

When asked why she carves, she replys, "I enjoy recreating in wood the beauty of birds that God has placed on earth for our enjoyment. So many people never get a chance to see birds in their natural habitat and they lose sight of the natural balance birds create."

Words of Wisdom: All work is for the birds, not the judges.

JIM SPRANKLE Professional

Black Duck Drake	1st
Gadwell Drake	1st
Shoveler Drake	1st
Cinnamon Teal Drake	1st
Ruddy Duck Drake	1st
Ringneck Drake	1st
Bufflehead Drake	2nd

Jim Sprankle has been a sucessful major league pitcher for the Brooklyn Dodgers and the Cincinnati Reds organizations, a banking executive and self-employed businessman.

Early age adventures in wildfowl hunting, combined with an ancestral woodworking background and experience as a self-taught taxidermist, have helped produce Jim's incredible knack for his life-like carvings. Indeed, two aviaries located at his home in Annapolis, Maryland, contain live birds of every specie of marsh ducks and many divers. The ability to observe these birds close at hand helps Jim to maintain a decided competitive edge in his carvings.

He began carving about 11 years ago and has become one of the best known carvers in the country. His carvings have earned him considerable recognition, including 18 Best of Show awards in major competitions throughout North America and over 60 First Place ribbons at the Ward Foundation World Championships.

Jim Sprankle and his wife, Patricia, have recently relocated to Annapolis, Maryland, within easy distance to the Chesapeake Bay and the Eastern Shore, thus realizing a life-long dream.

TOM STRAUSS Professional

Ruddy Drake	2nd
Wood Duck Drake	2nd
Blue Winged Teal Hen	3rd

Tom, his wife, Mary, and their 3 children all love carving and the friendly people associated with it.

His small aviary is used both as pets for the children and as models for carving decoys. He started carving competitively in 1980 and has been a judge at some contests including novice class in the 1984 World Championship.

Words of Wisdom: The most important element in carving a realistic decoy is to know what the live bird looks like. Don't start carving until you know what you are trying to carve.

BART WALTER Professional

Clapper Rails	3rd

Bart Walter, a Baltimore native, developed early a deep respect for waterbirds and Maryland's Eastern Shore. He began carving decoys in 1972 at the age of 14, and it has been a "love affair" ever since. In 1976, Bart entered college to study biology. At Hiram College, Bart managed an exotic waterfowl collection of over 40 species. This gave him the opportunity to study the behaviour and physiology of the birds, thus gaining new understanding and adding new dimensions to his carvings.

Since 1980, Bart has carved as a full time professional. Inspired by the paintings of Fuertes, Eckleberry, Clem, Liljefors and Bateman; Bart quickly became more interested in decorative bird sculpture, for he was then able to set a scene and create a mood. Everything, from the grasses waving in a breeze, to hermit crabs scuttling to their holes, to driftwood in the background, is hand made. This is done partly to get just the right look, but more importantly to increase durability, for Bart feels a great responsibility to produce long-lasting, high quality sculpture for his collectors.

JOY YAX Professional

Ruddy Duck	Second in
Drake Head	World
Grebe	1st

Joy, from Horsen's Island, Michigan, was a winner in two categories this year in addition to being a judge in another category and level.

Joy is among the first women to achieve the status of "judge" in the carving world.

GARY YODER Professional

Pheasants	1st and 3rd in show

Amateur

Carvers Biographies

L.R. AUKERMAN — Amateur

Emperor Goose	3rd in Confidence Class 1st in species all other Geese

A native of Pennsylvania would naturally love hunting and fishing and L.R. Aukerman is no exception. What started out as a hobby two years ago has earned him many ribbons in competition at Ocean City, a collection of waterfowl decoys and his very own aviary. Studying live birds can only enhance the carvers ability and building the aviary this year meant less time to spend on competition birds, but watch out in 1985.

Words of Wisdom: Study your subject and take no short cuts to achieve excellence.

BURT BARKER — Amateur

Common Loon 2nd

Burt is a secondary school and college science teacher who likes to concentrate his carving abilities on confidence birds. In the four short years he has been carving, the ribbons prove that his birds are well-liked by the judges. Each year he has entered the World Championships has brought him an award in the top three places as a novice or an amateur. 1984 was a special year at the U.S. Nationals when he swept the Open Class of Seabird Decoys, 1st, 2nd, and 3rd with Common and Artic Loons.

He credits his instructor, Paul McCarthy of Scituate, MA. as being a driving force to becoming a good carver.

Burts words of wisdom: Don't rush, be content with slow progress. Observe quietly and carefully, asking questions when needed. Work for form first and details will fall in place. Nothing can beat a top flight instructor. Above all, don't be discouraged.

TERRY BUCKWALTER — Amateur

Whimbrel (Miniature) 1st

Terry is a Quality Assurance Lab Supervisor who began his carving career by doing pen and ink drawings of birds. With encouragement from his father Harold, a carver also, he soon wanted to achieve the realism of carved birds. After a few "practice" birds he entered his first competition at the World Championship in 1982 and won a 1st and 3rd in show with his Godwit in novice class.

He carves 4 or 5 birds a year, now specializing in miniature shore birds, and considers his carving as a hobby at this time.

Attending good carving shows and seeing the fine work produced by todays top carvers have a big influence on his work.

PHIL BURKHART — Amateur

Black Duck 1st

Phil is from Newark, Delaware.

VIRGINIA "Betsy" CAMERON — Amateur

Canvasback Pair (Stained) 1st

Betsy is a native of Florida, and grew up with an intense interest in nature. Over the years, through studies, amateur "birding", conservation interests and painting, she has developed a deep love and respect for all the creatures and their habitats.

A self-taught carver, her inspiration has come from those who have already succeeded in capturing nature in all it's wonder and beauty.

Betsy's ribbons and awards from competitions the past couple of years include: blues and a first, second, and third "Best-in-Show" at the Mid-Atlantic Wildfowl Festival in Virginia Beach, a blue at the "World" Ocean City, Maryland and blues at other competitions.

Words of Wisdom: Study and learn as much as possible about your subjects in their habitat, from books and photos. Talk with other carvers. Most are glad to share tips and techniques. But mainly, get right in there and carve. Experience is a good teacher and builds needed confidence.

BERT CARTWRIGHT — Amateur

Ruddy Hen	1st
Ruddy Drake	2nd species
Mallard Drake	1st species and 3rd in category
Bufflehead Drake	1st species and 3rd in category

Bert has carved for three years. In that time he has won 12 first place ribbons as well as many 2nd and 3rd's. He is an avid hunter and has always admired carvings at shows. he enjoys all wildlife and has a special liking for the ducks.

Words of Wisdom: "Study the real birds and get help from experienced carvers".

JIM AND BETTY CUMMING — Amateur

Pigmy Owl with Chestnut Backed Chickadees 2nd

Jim and Betty as a team have been carving and painting wildfowl for the past five years. Jim, a native of NJ is a graduate of Syracuse University College of Forestry and was New Jersey's State Forester when he retired in 1983. He now carves full time.

Betty's home was in Kentucky and she began her career in the art world painting on canvas. Twenty years experience of flatwork artistry has helped her as she turned her talents to carving birds.

Both artists agree that attending seminars hosted by some of the country's leading carvers have enhanced their ablities. Belonging to organizations that support carving, such as the PA Delaware Valley Wood Carvers Association, and the Ward Foundation among others, is a way to find out what others are doing.

They exhibit at over two dozen shows annually and find the time to be judges at New Jersey's most prestigious event, the Middletown Wildlife Art and Decoy Competition.

Words of Wisdom: Acquire the best tools and reference materials available. Attend shows and support the organizations. Participate in classes and seminars, set high goals and seek your maxium potential.

CLIFF DUNLAP Amateur

Common Loon	1st and 1st in show
Avocet	2nd

Cliff is busy working on his degree in Electronics Engineering at Cleveland Institute, but still finds the time to carve blue ribbon birds.

Flatwork art held his interest, but 2-1/2 years ago he wanted to do something in a 3-dimensional scale. He entered a lifesize waterfowl head contest at the Ohio Duck and Decoy Show and won a 2nd place. Then in 1983 he placed 1st with a Ruffed Grouse and 2nd with a Canvasback Duck at the World championships at Ocean City.

Each year Cliff plans to finish higher in the competition and 1984 was proof of that.

"Nature is my influence and being the best carver I can is my goal."

Words of Wisdom: Observe and learn. Ask questions. Take it slow because there are no shortcuts. Research your bird and most of all have fun.

CURT FABRE Amateur

Green-Winged Teal	1st species, 2nd in marsh ducks

Curt Fabre developed his appreciation for wildlife growing up on the lower Bayou Terrebonne in the rural community of Montegut, Louisiana. He hunted with his father in the marshes over a set of Mark Whipple decoys purchased in 1928. This carver's workmanship kindled a desire in Curtis to try his hand at carving. He began carving decorative decoys for competition in 1979. Since then, he has won numerous awards including Best in Shows at Louisiana Wildfowl Festival in 1981, at Catahoula Lake Festival in 1981 and 82, at Cajun Hunters Festival 1983 and his recent Blue Ribbon prize at the World Championships in Ocean City, Maryland.

Curt's other hobbies include raising live waterfowl, collecting and researching to identify old working decoys from the bayou county. With his wife Cele, he operates an art and carvers supply shop at his home called "Curt's Waterfowl Corner".

Words of Wisdom: "Patience and determination is the name of the game."

D.J. FASKING Amateur

Pied Billed Grebe	2nd

D.J. is from Redford, New York.

EDNA FENTON Amateur

Carolina Wren	1st Song Bird Catagory

Edna's art form lies mainly in the carving and burning of tree fungus. In 1982 while attending the carving show in Clayton, N.Y., she became interested in bird carving. Her enthusiasm grew when in September 1983 she was able to spend a few hours in the studio of world champion, Ernie Muehlmatt.

Edna says "he graciously shared his expert knowlege with me and I give credit to him for having the greatest influence on my carving.

J.E. HAZELEY Amateur

Sage Grouse (Min.)	Third in World Miniatures
Wood Duck Family	1st and 2nd in Show
California Quail Pair	1st
Shootin' Stool Contest	Honorable Mention

Born and raised in Pennsylvania, he has worked as a product designer for Armstrong World Industries for 20 years. For 10 years before that he was an officer and pilot in the United States Navy. He holds a Bachelor of Design degree from the School of Architecture and Fine Art from the University of Florida.

Although he only recently turned to waterfowl as a medium, they have always been a favorite theme for him. He's been observing them for years. Eight to ten years ago, however, he attended a small carving show where he saw the work of Ernie Muehlmatt. Although he was amazed by the excellence of these carvings and ones he saw at other shows, he found himself a bit intimated as an artist himself.

He began carving in 1981 and entered his first competition in 1983 at the World Championship. He has consistantly won ribbons since then. He has carvings in several private collections. He is a member of Cornell University Laboratory of Ornithology, The Ward Foundation, Ducks Unlimited, the National Wildlife Federation, the Smithsonian Institution, the American Museum of Natural History and the Lancaster County Woodcarvers Association.

Words of Wisdom: "Never be afraid to try. Your carving may not be a Blue Ribbon Winner, but I'm willing to bet it'll be better than you thought it would be and the next one will be better yet."

ROBERT C. JAMEISON Amateur

Cinnamon Teal	1st
Shoveler	1st
Blue Wing Teal	2nd

Robert began carving because of a great love for wildlife. With help from his fellow carvers, artists, and the support of his wife, he has been able to accomplish much in this art form. Having started serious carving in 1981, Robert won his first World Championship Award in 1982. Since that time, he has won numerous awards in many shows, including 2 first, 1 second, and 3 honorable mentions in the 1984 World Championship.

Words of Wisdom: Patience, perseverance, and dedication make a good carver; without it, you are your own greatest obstacle.

RON KAGARISE — Amateur

Kestrel (Miniature)	1st Birds of Prey 2nd Best-in-show Amateur Min.
Ruffed Grouse (Miniature)	1st
King Fisher	2nd

Retiring in 1983 after a long career with the Federal Government, Ron now looks forward to more time for carving.

He became interested in wildfowl carving after attending the Easton Waterfowl Festival and produced his first decoy in 1978. This was a natural outgrowth of longstanding activities in birding, photography and oil painting.

In 1981 he was a novice and a winner of four ribbons, including a 2nd best-of-show, at the World championship. As an amateur in 1983 his four miniature carvings garnered 5 ribbons, with another 2nd best-in-show.

Concentrating on miniature waterfowl was Ron's main interest early in his career, but he has since expanded his talents to other kinds of wildfowl.

Words of Wisdom: Carver! Know thy bird.

DICK LEDFORD — Amateur

Blue-Winged Teal	1st
Green-Winged Teal	Honorable Mention
Bufflehead (shooting stool)	Honorable Mention

Dick began carving waterfowl about 6 years ago. He has participated in several national carving workshops sponsored by the Ward Foundation. Dick has entered his carvings in national contests in New York, Maryland, Louisianna, California, Michigan, Iowa, and Canada. During the last three years his carvings have won 10 blue ribbons including first and second places in the 1982 Canadian National Exhibition in Toronto.

Dick holds a PhD from Cornell University and has been a professor at Cornell since 1964. He and his wife, Martha, and the youngest of their five children live in Ithaca, New York.

Words of Wisdom: Beginners, in my opinion, should do a lot of research on the species they plan to carve. Determination to do a good job is important. Much is learned by attending competitions, especially The World Championships, sponsored by the Ward Foundation.

PENELOPE MACE — Amateur

Baird's Cormorant	2nd

Penny was born into a military family in Yonkers, New York, raised in El Paso, Texas, and now resides in Cecil County, Maryland. She had never really noticed ducks, much less decoys, until moving to the upper Chesapeake Bay area 10 years ago. She says once she noticed them, it was love at first sight! She began carving in 1978 and has carved steadily as a hobby ever since.

She mixes carving time with a busy schedule of raising two sons, helping maintain a farm, occasional errand running for their tire and exhaust business and educating the mathematical minds of the students of the nearby high school.

Her entire family enjoys this consuming hobby with she and her sons winning ribbons in national competition and her husband carving cartoon ducks.

BOB MANNING — Amateur

Loon	1st
Blue-Winged Teal	1st
Wood Duck	Honorable Mention

RUSSELL MARTIN JR. — Amateur

Gadwall Drake	1st species, 1st marshducks, 3rd in show

Russell is 19 years old and lives in Chauvin, Louisiana, along bayou "Petit Caillou". He has competed for three years and has won many blue ribbons. He won Best in Show novice at the "LWCCG" Show and Best in Show amateur at the Catahoula Lake Festival". His father is his greatest critic and influence.

WENDY MICHAEL — Amateur

Common Loon (miniature)	1st and 3rd Best in Show
Yellowlegs	Honorable Mention
Flicker Feather	Honorable Mention

Wendy, who was born and raised in Canada, has always been close to birds and wildlife. After graduating from a commercial art course at Danforth Technical School in 1961, she became involved in the printing business and now operates her own silk screen print shop.

She began studying bird carving in 1980 with Paul Burdette and presently is represented by the Burdette Wildlife Gallery, Orton, Ontario.

Wendy's list of ribbons are numerous from the contests she has entered in both the U.S. and Canada. She actively supports Ducks Unlimited by contributing a bird each year to their auction. In 1985 Wendy will use her carving talents to begin teaching others.

PAIGE C. PAULSON — Amateur

Bobwhite Quail Stained	1st

Paige was a winner at the 1983 World Championship, placing 3rd in the Novice category with a Lifesize Ring-necked Pheasant. Moving up to Amateur status in 1984 brought a Blue Ribbon to the Quail.

"My goal is to become one of the best wildlife sculpture artists."

JOHN E. PHELAN — Amateur

Goldeneye (Drake)	1st
Bluebill (Drake)	1st

In less than two years John has won over 20 awards, all with only the five birds he has carved. A best of show in California and at the C.N.E. helped to make him the professional that he is.

He credits his success to the help and guidance of fellow carvers and his knowledge of the birds he is carving.

Words of Wisdom: The best advice a carver can give has little to do with technique or methods. The most important aspect in carving a bird is to know the bird you are attempting to carve.

ERWIN W. PILLSBURY — Amateur

Ringneck Duck (Drake)	1st
Shootin' Stool	Honorable Mention

Carving seven decoys in three years has earned Erwin a total of twenty awards, eleven of them Blue Ribbons.

He enjoys going to the competitions to meet other carvers. "Talking with them and learning from them has been a big influence in my carvings", says Erwin. "I would like to become a better carver and get more non-carvers interested in the art."

Words of Wisdom: I believe in attending the decoy contests to see what other carvers are doing, talking to the professionals for helpful hints, and getting all the reference material you can on the subject you're carving are all important.

JAN G. REESE

Amateur

Little Tern (Min.)	Honorable Mention
3 Sanderlings	1st
Cormorant (Min. Stained)	Honorable Mention

Jan began carving in 1984 with encouragement and guidance from Esther and Ed Burns. Competing in the World Championship permitted her direct comparison of her work with work of other carvers, while providing a test of her first efforts in this sculptured art medium.

Jan finds that receiving ribbons, admiration and encouragement from other carvers is certainly incentive to continue carving.

FRANK RYAN

Amateur

Loon	1st
Black Duck (Shootin' Stool)	Honorable Mention

Carving and donating a few decorative duck decoys to a chapter of Ducks Unlimited started Frank on his way to carving for competition. After attending the World Championship contest in 1983, he decided to go home and do some serious carving. He came back this year and won a Blue Ribbon.

Attending the seminars given each Spring by the Ward Foundation and reading good carving books have helped him improve. He has not taken any formal carving courses. His goal is to be the best carver possible.

Words of Wisdom: When possible, get all carving information from the real bird.

ROBERT ALLEN SAKUTA

Amateur

Canada Goose	1st, 1st category 2nd in Show

Robert is from Livonia, Michigan.

WILLARD E. SHANTZ

Amateur

Kestrel	1st
Lapwing (Miniature)	2nd
Yellow Throated Warbler	Honorable Mention

Williard is a graduate of the Ontario Veterinary College, Guelph, Ontario and is now district veterinarian with Agriculture Canada in Barrie, Ontario, having previously practiced in large and small animal medicine as well as zoo animal medicine. His avocation has been the study of birds since a very early age both through the observation of birds in the wild and his interest in aviculture.

His addiction to bird carving started about five years ago. Willard has studied under Paul Burdette and Bob Ptashnik and has accumulated over thirty-five ribbons and awards at various competitions.

He has found realistic bird carving a wonderful form of relaxation and challenge and a means to express his deep interest in birds.

Words of wisdom: Never be fully satisfied with your carving, there is always room for improvement. Make every effort to become fully familiar with the species you are carving. Through studying and observing the live birds, reading life histories, and studying photographs, you will develop a profile of the bird's anatomy, behaviour, unique peculiarities and demeanor.

JIM SHERMAN

Amateur

Brown Thrasher (Min.)	1st and Best in Show
Common Tern	1st and 2nd in Show
Feather (Lady Amherst Pheasant)	Best in World

Jim is a 44 year-old patent attorney for Rockwell International. To him carving is a serious part-time hobby. He is already planning to enter and win the World Miniature Class in 1986 and the World Lifesize Decoratives in 1987. It's very possible the he will win, because he has carved the Best Feather in the World Championship for the past 3 years. Jim also has Blue Ribbons in the Canadian National Decoy contest, North American Decoy Carving Championship, Southwestern Pennsylvania Water Fowlers contest, and of course the World Championship.

Although Jim has never taken any lessons, he credits the valuable advice and suggestions he gets from many experienced carvers for his success. He began carving almost 4 1/2 years ago.

When his children are educated and on their own, Jim would like to begin carving full time.

Words of Wisdom: Enter the feather carving contest. It is one competition where the Judge can look at the "real" feather and compare it to yours. It will improve your carving, burning and painting skills.

HERB WATSON

Amateur

Bird	Place
Pintail Drake	1st
Canada Geese (Min.)	Honorable Mention

Herb, a native of the Eastern Shore Region, has been carving birds for four years. Working at the William B. Tilghman Company gives him time to carve birds as a hobby only, but some day he hopes to make it a full time profession.

His first competition in September, 1982 at the Mid-Atlantic Waterfowl Festival at Virginia Beach, Virginia won him a Third Place Ribbon and since then he has won awards at the Easter Decoy Show in Chincoteague, Virginia and the World Championship at Ocean City, Maryland.

Herb has also exhibited at the Easton, Maryland Waterfowl Festival.

TOM WEBB

Amateur

Bird	Place
Hooded Merganser (Drake)	1st and 2nd Best Diver
Mallard	2nd

Tom, who was born and raised in Michigan, has been a patternmaker for 34 years.

He has won numerous ribbons and plaques since beginning carving 3 years ago. He has entered the competitions at the North American Wildfowl Carving Championship, Canadian National Decoy Contest and the World Championship, where his birds have always done well.

His goal is to carve top quality decoys and to help further wildfowl art appreciation.

Words of Wisdom: Do your research and pay close attention to detail.

Novice

Carvers Biography

GEORGE K. AGARDI, II — Novice

Surf Scoter — 1st

George is a 24 year old teacher of Industrial Arts on Long Island. He has made decoys for the past twelve years but the 1984 World Championship was the first show he competed in. He was introduced to carving by a friend of his who is no longer with us, Len Tucker who worked only with three pen knives.

W.J. "MICK" BRAZELL — Novice

Lesser Scaup — 1st and 2nd Diver

Mick originally began carving hunting decoys in the late 1950s, basically copying the work of the Schmidts, Meldrums, Walters, and Schrams (being from the St. Clair flats area) and studying wild birds which abound in this area.

After a twenty year career in the U.S. Navy he returned to this area and rekindled his interest in decoys. He has virtually started over as a decoy maker (the World Show was his third contest, Point Moulee 2nd place, Toronto 3rd place, World Show 1st place species 2nd place Diver). He hopes to increase his knowledge and abilities to where he can compete with today's group of skilled carvers.

Words of Wisdom: Obtain all the reference material you possibly can and observe your subject in the wild whenever possible.

ANTHONY CHRISTOFICH — Novice

Brant — Blue

Anthony has been a carpenter for 28 years and a duck carver for two. His favorite hobby is working with wood, as he puts it, "from desks to ducks". He has carved over 50 ducks to date which have won many awards including several first place ribbons.

Words of Wisdom: "To be a successfull carver, one should persevere with a specific interest and develope that skill with practice."

RICHARD CORR — Novice

Wigeon — 1st

Richard is from Dewitt, Michigan.

TROY DANOS — Novice

Redhead — 1st and 3rd in Show Diver
Pintail — 3rd

At the age of 16, you might say Troy is a chip off the old block. He credits his father Carl as the man who most influences him and teaches him about carving. Each day they work together is a day closer to the goal Troy has set for himself. To win Best Teenage carver and then to master carver.

After competing for only three years and winning many ribbons, he considers his wins at the world competition as the most honorable in his career.

Words of Wisdom: Don't get discouraged with your first carving. Learn from your mistakes. Competition makes you better. Ask the master carvers for advice.

HAMILTON N. DANTIN — Novice

Coot — 1st
Widgeon Drake — 2nd
Widgeon Hen — 3rd
Pintail Drake — Honorable Mention

1981 was the year another carver started on his way to blue ribbons. Hamilton began with a simple gunning stool and a lot of help from a good friend, Richard Wagespack. After attending a few shows he knew that decorative birds were what he wanted to carve.

Sharing knowledge is a carvers code and he credits another great carver, Willie Badeaux, with more help than he could ever imagine. "I can never repay what I've learned from him".

His ribbons for 1982 totaled 15, including Best-of-Show. 1983 brought 18 awards and first time ever at the "World" in 1984 he took home 4 ribbons.

Hamilton will become a professional carver in 1985.

DALE R. DINSE — Novice

Ruddy Drake — 1st in species
1st in category
Best-in-Show
Shoveler — 2nd

Dale has accomplished a goal that he set for himself just two years ago. Winning a blue ribbon at the "World" competition as a novice carver after carving only three birds proves that his determination paid off. His other birds a bufflehead and a shoveler, also won awards at shows in Canada and Michigan. He plans to continue sculpting waterfowl and someday hopes to become a professional carver.

Dale says "my artistic abilities have been a satisfying personal resource which I not only enjoy as a hobby, but are very much involved in my everyday life as well."

Words of Wisdom: The beginning carver should attain his own style. Patience is a virtue which all carvers must possess. Keep in mind that nothing is too difficult if you want it badly enough.

PAUL DOHERTY — Novice

Hooded Merganser Drake — 1st

Paul is from East Northport, New York.

BOB DOWNS — Novice

Shoveler Drake — 1st

Bob's three year carving experience made him decide that 1984 would be the year to enter competition. The Virginia Beach Show brought him a 1st place Shoveler ribbon, a 2nd place Bufflehead, and a 3rd place Lesser Scaup.

He credits his good fortune to his classes at the Craftwoods and his weekend instruction at Veasey Studios.

Bob has set a goal to be one of the best full-time blue ribbon professional carvers in competition. His motto: "Go for the blue" is a direct quote from Bill Veasey.

Words of Wisdom: Study the bird you want to carve. Reference material and good advice are a must. Your carving should have no flat sides; it should follow flow lines. A good carving has soft, smooth feathers and a sharp, clean painted finish. Never, never say "I can't."

JOHN P. ENGLISH — Novice

Eider Duck Drake — 1st

John is from East Orleans, Massachusetts.

JIM B. GANLEY

Bufflehead	1st
Lesser Scaup Hen	3rd
Canvasback	Honorable Mention
Redhead	Honorable Mention

Jim started carving about 3 years ago and truly loves his hobby. His first bird in competition won him a Blue Ribbon. Since that first blue he's added 10 other awards in later contests.

Jim hopes "some day to win the BIG one. I'll keep trying because this is really a challenge."

Words of Wisdom: Don't give up.

E.J. HAM — Novice

Gadwall — 1st

Words of Wisdom: Take a seminar from someone who knows what they are doing! A six-day seminar with Bill Veasey did more for my carving than two years of "piddling" on my own.

CAROL KINNEY — Novice

Wood Duck	1st and 3rd in class
Woodcock	1st
Pied-Billed Grebe	2nd
Horned Grebe	Honorable Mention
Kestrel	Honorable Mention

Carol began entering competitions in 1984, and her birds have done well. She has been carving for four years and now conducts carving classes with her partner Don McKinlay from their studio, *"The Feather Merchants.*

EDWARD R. MICHALIK — Novice

Canvasback Hen — Blue

Words of Wisdom: "Go to the best carving instructor you can afford. Get all the information you can on the subject. Get photo's. Ask questions. Do the very best you can and, above all, Be class!"

JEFFREY MUHS — Novice

Black Duck	1st and 2nd Best Marsh Duck
Red-Breasted Merganser Drake	1st

Jeff, who has been carving birds for nine years, carved his first duck at the age of eight. Since that first attempt, he has constantly improved.

Jeff's Black Duck in 1984 was Best of Show, U.S. National Decoy Show on Long Island, 1st place, Novice, 2nd best Marsh Duck in 1984 World Championship. He has won the E. Tanner Fraser Memorial award at the World Show for the last two years for the most outstanding teenage carver.

His future education will be in the art field and he will be spending his summer carving in his father's wildlife gallery in Westhampton Beach, New York.

Words of Wisdom: No matter what your age, with proper instruction and dedication, your carvings will improve with each attempt.

JOHN D. PERSONETTE — Novice

Mallard Drake	1st
Blue-Winged Teal Hen	2nd

JANET SOMEROFF — Novice

Goldeneye Drake — 1st

Janet was a pianist, appearing on television and in concerts on both the east and west coasts.

Her late husband Ben, a well-known still life photographer and Janet's most important influence, persuaded her to begin carving. Ben's influence inspired Janet to do her best and to continually improve her work.

Janet carved her first "fantasy bird" out of walnut in 1981, consequently appearing on the cover of *Handy Man.* In late 1981 she started taking a waterfowl carving class with Ken Gleason. In the summer of 1982, she studied songbird carving with Mary Worrilow.

Her current goal is to "enter the art that is beyond shape and feathers".

Words of Wisdom: Practice *really* seeing birds; do not make mental assumptions. Before you can interpret, if you do so, you must know your subject.

JACK WALKER — Novice

Green-Winged Teal Hen — 1st

Jack has been carving for about 3 years. 1984 was his first win at the World Championship. His other ribbons have been at the Midwest Decoy Show in Detroit, Michigan.

Jack is a Certified Public Accountant with his own practice in Michigan.

Index